OUR PEOPLE

HISTORY OF THE JEWS

VOL. I

BOOKS 1-2

OUR PEOPLE

History of the Jews

A Text Book of Jewish History for the School and Home

by
JACOB ISAACS

Volume I
Book 1 & 2

Published and Copyright by
MERKOS L'INYONEI CHINUCH
770 Eastern Parkway
Brooklyn, New York 11213

5751 • 1991

CONTENTS OF VOLUME I

SUPPLEMENT

ILLUSTRATIONS

FOREWORD

There has long been a pressing need for a textbook of Jewish History in English, faithfully adhering to the spirit of the Scriptures, for the Jewish school and home. The need has been especially felt in those quarters where it is realized that a textbook of Jewish History must be free from anti-religious bias, or any tendency to lower the sanctity of the Torah.

It is with a view to providing a textbook of Jewish History that would be acceptable to all Jewish schools, Yeshivoth and Talmud Torahs, as well as to all the Jewish homes where the traditions of our people are still carefully preserved — acceptable because of its spirit of loyalty to the sacred heritage of our people, because of its accent on the didactic value of our history, and finally because of its clear and suitable style — that the MERKOS L'INYONEI CHINUCH has undertaken the publication of this and the coming volumes of the history of OUR PEOPLE.

The innovation of the present textbook (if indeed it may be termed "innovation") lies in the fact that the presentation of the Bible narrative in these volumes has been complemented by our other traditional sources, such as the Talmud and Midrash.

Throughout the presentation of this textbook runs an unbroken "thread of blue" — that it is Divine Providence that is guiding the destiny of our people; that this destiny is closely linked to the great mission and task of our people as "a kingdom of priests and a holy nation," a task which is binding not only to our entire people as a whole, but to each individual member as well.

Thus the Jewish child studying Jewish history out of this textbook will do more than learn to feel the pride and dignity of being a Jew or Jewess; for by better understanding the true meaning of our history of yesterday the child will more fully appreciate the history-making events of our life today and tomorrow. This will enable him, when he grows up, to readily find the answer to many a perplexing question besetting the minds of men and women of our age.

BROOKLYN, N. Y., 1946   JACOB ISAACS

I. THE BEGINNING OF MANKIND

1. CREATION OF THE WORLD

**THE
CREATION:** The word of G-d brought everything into being: heaven and earth, mountains and rivers, and every living thing. In the beginning, G-d called into existence the heaven and earth. Within six days He shaped a world of order and beauty.

**THE
FIRST DAY:** On the first day, G-d said: "Let there be Light"—and there was Light.

**THE
SECOND DAY:** On the second day G-d made the sky, and called it Heaven.

**THE
THIRD DAY:** On the third day, G-d put the earth into good shape. At His command the waters of the earth gathered together at certain places. The waters formed seas and oceans, lakes and rivers, so that in other parts, the dry land became visible.

At G-d's further command, the earth was made to produce all kinds of plants, grass, and trees, shrubs and flowers. Each contained its own seed for further growth and reproduction.

**THE
FOURTH DAY:** On the fourth day, G-d made the Sun, the Moon, and the Stars, to shed light upon the earth. And so He set a time for day and a time for night, a time for the week, the month, and the year, and a time for each of the four seasons.

**THE
FIFTH DAY:** On the fifth day, G-d filled the seas with fishes and other water animals. Into the air above the earth He put many birds of all kinds and colors and sizes.

**THE
SIXTH DAY:** On the sixth day, were created all the other animals, large and small, those that walk and those that creep or crawl on the earth. And towards the end of the sixth day, G-d put a divine soul into a body which He made of earth and clay. This was Man. To him G-d granted high mental ability so that he could think and reach his own conclusions. G-d also gave Man the power of speech and so He made him superior to all the other creatures of the earth. G-d put all the creatures of the earth and the powers of nature in the control of Man.

**THE
SEVENTH DAY:** By the seventh day, everything was created and put into shape and order. And G-d rested on the seventh day and He glorified it as a day of rest. And so, we should work for six days and rest on the Seventh day, Shabos, which G-d blessed and sanctified for all time to come. By observing the Shabbos day, we show that we believe in G-d as the Creator of the world.

2. THE FIRST HUMAN BEINGS AND THE GARDEN OF EDEN

**THE FIRST MAN
AND WOMAN:** Adam ("man of earth"), was the name of the first human being whom G-d formed out of soil taken from all parts of the earth.

Then, G-d created tht first woman—Eve, to be Adam's wife.

G-D'S BLESSING: G-d blessed Adam and Eve, saying: "Be fruitful and multiply, cultivate the earth, and control it. Rule over the fish of the sea, and over the birds of the air, and over every living thing that moves on the earth!"

THE GARDEN OF EDEN: And Adam and Eve lived happily in "Gan Eden," the Garden of Delight, which was the best part of the entire globe. They did not have to exert themselves to get their food, for everything was aplenty in the Garden of Eden.

THE SERPENT: But the happiness of Adam and Eve in the Garden of Eden was not to last long. For, together with them, lived also the Serpent which was shrewder than all the other animals. The Serpent begrudged G-d's blessing given to Adam and Eve. He envied them the power to rule over the creatures of the world. He, therefore, devised a scheme by which to make the first human beings fall.

THE FIRST COMMANDMENT: When G-d gave Adam permission to eat the fruits of all the trees in the Garden of Eden, He warned him not to eat of the fruit of the "Etz Hadaath," the Tree of Knowledge of good and evil, which stood in the middle of the Garden. Its fruits were very beautiful. As long as Adam did not eat of it, he was like an angel who does only good and lives forever. The fruit of the "Etz Hadaath," however, had the power to fill a man with the desire for both good and evil.

THE PLOT: The Serpent, knowing this fact, based his plan on it. He met Eve alone in the Garden and asked her cunningly: "Is it true that G-d really told you, 'You shall not eat the fruit of every tree in the Garden?' "

"Oh, no," answered the woman. "We may eat the fruit of all the trees in the Garden. But of the fruit of the tree which is in the middle of the Garden, G-d has said, 'You shall not eat it, nor touch it, lest you die!' " But the serpent said: "You will not die. G-d knows very well that when you eat the fruit of this tree your eyes will be opened, and you will be like G-d, Who knows both good and evil."

THE FIRST SIN: Eve looked at the tree. Its fruit looked good to eat, pleasant and attractive. But her heart warned her not to give up eternal life for the sake of power and pleasure. She was torn between her desire to eat and her fear of death, and she could not resist the temptation. She not only ate of the fruit herself, but she also gave some of it to Adam, so that he would have to share her fate.

THEIR EXCUSE: Suddenly, Adam and Eve heard G-d's voice in the Garden, and they were afraid. They hid behind the trees and bushes. But G-d called to Adam: "Where art thou?" Adam replied: "I heard Thy voice in the Garden and became afraid."

"Hast thou eaten of the tree which I commanded thee not to eat of?" said G-d. Adam replied: "I am not guilty. The woman Thou hast given me as a companion gave me some fruit of the tree, and I ate it."

Then G-d asked Eve why she had done so, and she too had an excuse, saying that the Serpent had tricked her and made her eat of the Tree of Good and Evil.

THE PUNISHMENT: Then G-d turned to the Serpent and said: "Because thou hast done this, cursed art thou from among all creatures, and from among all beasts of the field; upon thy belly shalt thou go, and dust shalt thou eat all the days of thy life. And I shall put hatred between thee and the woman and between thy offspring and her children; they shall crush thy head, and thou shalt sting their heel."

To the woman G-d said: "Thy pain and thy trouble will be very great; thou shalt bear children in pain; and thy husband shall rule over thee."

To Adam G-d said: "Because thou hast listened to the voice of thy wife, and hast eaten of the tree which I commanded thee not to eat of, cursed be the ground for thy sake; with labor shalt thou eat of it all the days of thy life. Thorns and thistles shall it bring forth to thee; and thou shalt eat the herb of the field. In the sweat of thy face shalt thou eat bread, till thou returnest to the ground, for out of it wast thou taken; for dust thou art, and unto dust shalt thou return."

EXPULSION FROM THE GARDEN OF EDEN: Then G-d drove Adam and Eve out of the Garden of Eden where they had had everything they needed and desired without trouble. Adam and Eve now had to work; they had to till the soil in order to get food for themselves.

3. CAIN AND ABEL

ADAM'S CHILDREN: The first human beings to be born were Cain and Abel, the two children of Adam and Eve.

CAIN'S JEALOUSY: Cain, the first-born, was a tiller of the soil, and Abel became a shepherd. Cain was always busy, toiling to get food from the earth, which refused to grow of its own accord as it used to in the days before Adam and Eve's sin. Abel, however, spent much of his time thinking about his parents' mistake, and of ways of making amends for it. In a spirit of repentance and gratitude Abel brought some of his best young lambs as an offering to G-d. Cain saw this, and he, too, wanted to offer something to G-d. He, therefore, selected the most exquisite first fruits of the year as his offering. But Cain's offering was not accepted by G-d because he did not give it wholeheartedly and of his own free will, as Abel did. When Cain observed that G-d did not care for his offering, he became angry at his brother and decided to kill him.

CAIN IS WARNED: G-d, the All-seeing, the All-merciful, reproved him gently. He asked him why he was angry, and why his countenance was fallen. If his offering was not accepted, should he not take it as a sure sign that he had not done well? He ought to take heed, or repentance would come too late.

THE MURDER OF ABEL: Cain discussed this with his brother. While they were in the midst of talking over what is right and what is wrong, Cain rose against his brother and killed him. When G-d asked him where Abel was, he answered, "I do not know. Am I my brother's keeper?"

CAIN'S PUNISHMENT: G-d said to Cain, "What hast thou done? The voice of thy brother's blood crieth unto Me from the ground. And now art thou more cursed than the ground; henceforth it shall not yield her strength unto thee; thou shalt be a fugitive and a wanderer over the earth."

CAIN'S REPENTANCE: Cain was sorry for doing his evil deed and he prayed to G-d to make his punishment lighter: "My punishment is greater than I can bear. Behold, Thou hast this day driven me away from the land; and from Thy face I shall be hid and I shall be fugitive and a wanderer over the earth; and it shall come to pass that whosoever meets me will slay me." Thus pleaded Cain, and his desperate plea was heard. G-d assured Cain that nobody would kill him until the seventh generation. And a sign appeared on Cain's forehead to serve as a warning that nobody should kill him.

CAIN'S CHILDREN: Cain wandered all over the earth, till he finally settled in Nod, "the land of wandering," east of Eden. He had many, many children. They multiplied and were powerful One of the last descendants of Cain was Yabal, the first man to live in a tent and to raise cattle. Another descendant was Yubal, who was the first to play the lyre and the flute. Another was Tubal-Cain, who was the first man to make tools out of metal. Tubal-Cain had a sister Naamah.

CAIN'S DEATH: Tubal-Cain's father, the sixth generation from Cain, was Lemech. Lemech grew old and became blind. One day Tubal-Cain, his youngest son, led him out into the fields to hunt for food. Far off, Tubal-Cain saw something moving that looked like a monstrous animal. He advised the blind Lemech to aim his arrow towards it, and Lemech shot. When they got closer, they discovered to their great sorrow that they had killed Cain.

4. ADAM'S DESCENDANTS

ADAM'S DEATH: Adam had a third son Seth, who was to become the father of all future generations of man.

Adam died at the age of nine hundred and thirty years. His death was mourned by all human beings. He and his wife were buried in the Cave of Machpelah, near Hebron, (in the land of Israel).

SETH'S CHILDREN: During the life of Seth's son Enosh, people began to make images and statues to remind them of G-d. Later, however, the people began to worship the idols they had made. And so, they turned away from G-d, and neglected the laws of right conduct which G-d had given to Adam. G-d saw the evil doings of the new generation and punished it time and again by sending great floods which destroyed a third of all the people living, and by causing other disasters such as famines and epidemics. But, none of these warnings brought the people to their senses.

ENOCH: Only in the time of Enoch (Chanoch), who was the seventh generation removed from Adam, did men improve their conduct. Enoch devoted all his life and work to the service of G-d. He lived for many years a life of isolation and prayer. When he returned to live among the people, they soon recognized his great wisdom and justice, and elected him their leader. Under his rule there was peace all over the world. He restored faith and law among the people, so that no one stole from his neighbor, or robbed the traveler.

This order lasted till the year 930, when Adam died. Then Enoch again withdrew into seclusion, appearing only occasionally to give advice to the people and to answer the questions that had arisen during the period of his absence. Enoch did not die like any other human beings. He was one of the few whom G-d took away alive.

METHUSELAH: During the life on Enoch's son, Methuselah (who lived nine hundred and sixty-nine years, longer than any other human being), the people again revolted against G-d, and there prevailed a state of lawlessness, cruelty, and corruption that brought doom and destruction upon the world.

5. NOAH AND THE FLOOD

THE WICKEDNESS OF THE PEOPLE: Methuselah's w i s d o m and knowledge were inherited by his grandson Noah, the son of Lemech. Noah was a righteous and pious man.

When Noah was five hundred years old, he had three sons—Shem, Ham, and Japheth. They too were good and pious men, fearing and loving G-d, and unlike all the other inhabitants of the earth, who had gradually become more and more depraved. Yet neither Noah nor Methuselah could change the evil ways of the people around them, in spite of the many warnings G-d sent through them to their fellow-men. Everyone thought only of his own welfare and recognized only the laws that were in his own favor. Mutual respect and cooperation had given way to violence and sin.

Finally G-d gave them a last chance. He ordered Noah to build an ark slowly, and to complete it in one hundred and twenty years. This was to be the last period of grace within which the people could change their evil ways. Time passed and yet the people had not repented. So fearful was the prevailing corruption that G-d determined to destory all life by a universal Deluge; not only the men but the beasts also were to perish, so that no trace might remain of that wicked age.

Only Noah found grace in the eyes of G-d, and he was to be spared the fate of all the other living things, because he was the only pious person who had tried to arouse the conscience of the people and warn them of the punishment to come.

THE ARK: G-d told Noah to build his ark in public and to tell everyone its purpose: that it would save him from the coming Flood. The Ark was to be three hundred cubits in length, fifty in width, and thirty in height, and was to consist of three stories, divided into small rooms to hold people, animals, and food. Noah and his wife, their three sons, Shem, Ham, and Japheth, and their wives were to live in it. Some animals of every kind in the world were to live in the Ark too, Noah's family and the animals were to live in the Ark until the Flood ended. Noah did as G-d commanded. His neighbors made fun of him for his faith, and they paid no attention to his warnings of the Flood that was to come.

THE FLOOD: Noah was six hundred year old when G-d told him to go into the Ark with his whole family, and to admit the animals which G-d had selected.

The Flood commenced on the seventeenth day of the second month. The gates of heaven broke loose, and the depths of the earth opened to send forth streams of raging, boiling water, swallowing everything in its path. Rain fell for forty days and forty nights and the water which covered the earth rose higher and higher. It covered the peaks of the highest mountains. Every living thing died, and all growing things were destroyed. Amid this terrible scene of ruins and devastation the Ark, guided by G-d, floated securely. But the ship was fiercly tossed about and shaken at the heights of the stormy flood, so that it seemed to Noah that it was about to break apart.

THE FLOOD RECEDES: Noah and his children prayed constantly, and at last the flood quieted down. A wind blew over the earth and the Ark came to rest upon the mountains of Ararat, after it had been afloat for seven months.

THE RAVEN AND THE DOVE: Gradually the water subsided; and on the first day of the tenth month the peaks of the mountains could be seen again. Noah, still imprisoned in the Ark, looked forth upon the widespreading though decreasing waters; and after waiting forty days longer, he sent forth a raven from the Ark. This bird, glad to regain and to enjoy its liberty, returned to the Ark only to be fed, flitting to and fro, until the waters had quite abated. Yet, Noah, anxiously hoping that the floods were disappearing from the land, sent out another bird, and this time a dove. But the dove, more delicate than the raven, found no resting place, and returned to the Ark. After seven days it was again sent forth, and now it returned at eventime with a fresh olive leaf in its mouth. Then Noah knew that the earth was almost free from the flood, although still unfit for habitation. After another seven days, the winged messenger was sent out again and returned no more. A feeling of gladness must in truth have filled Noah's heart, for in the beginning of the first month, the surface of the earth was cleared from the waters, and three hundred and sixty-five days after the commencement of the Flood, the ground was perfectly dry.

The Flood had passed, but it had changed the appearance of the earth and of the entire universe. Everything, even the light of the sun, had lost some of its original strength and power, and the earth was barren and unyielding.

NOAH'S OFFERING: Noah and his family spent a whole year in the Ark. Then G-d ordered them to leave the Ark. Noah built an altar and brought an offering which G-d accepted graciously. And G-d promised that He would never again curse the earth because of man. Seasons, heat and cold, day and night, and all the other laws of nature would never again fail altogether, as they had done in the time of the Flood.

THE SEVEN LAWS: G-d blessed Noah and his sons with the same blessing He had given Adam and Eve, giving them power over all living creatures. Before, they had been allowed to eat only herbs and plants. Now they were allowed to use meat for food, but only after the animal had been killed. To eat flesh torn from a living animal was forbidden. And stern was His decree against the shedder of human blood. Murder was to be unsparingly avenged by death; for could a greater crime be conceived than that of destroying a being created by G-d in His own image? Other commandments were, the establishment of Courts of Justice, the prohibition of blasphemy, indecency, idolatry, and robbery.

G-D'S COVENANT WITH NOAH: These rules G-d included in a treaty with Noah and Noah's sons. As a sign of the Covenant G-d showed them a rainbow up in the clouds, as a permanent record for all times to come.

6. NOAH'S CHILDREN

HAM'S SIN: Noah began to till the soil, and he planted a vineyard. One day he drank some of the wine, not knowing its strength, and he became drunk. Seeing his father lying drunk in his tent, Ham told his brothers about it in a very rude way. His two brothers went into the tent, where they covered their father and put him in his bed without looking at him in his shame. When Noah awoke and found out what had happened, he was angry at his son Ham, saying that Ham's children should be slaves to the children of his brothers Shem and Japheth.

Then he prayed that Shem and Japheth have wisdom and beauty, and great social and cultural achievements.

SHEM AND HIS DESCENDANTS: Shem became a prophet of G-d and lived six hundred years, serving G-d as a priest. In the time of Abraham, who was the ninth generation in direct line of descent from Shem, Shem was famous under the name of Malkitzedek, the "Just King," who brought offerings to G-d. He lived to see the eleventh generation of his descendants (Jacob). Together with his worthy great-grandson Eber, he taught and spread faith in G-d and in His commands in a school which was known as the Academy of Shem and Eber.

During the time of Eber's son Peleg, the lifespan of human beings dwindled down to about one half of what it was in the former generation.

7. THE TOWER OF BABEL

**CONCEIT OF
THE PEOPLE:**
It was towards the end of Peleg's life that something happened which changed the social life of all men on earth.

After the Flood, man had again begun to multiply and fill the earth. They all spoke one language and understood one another well. The generations of people before the Flood had been interested only in themselves; they thought of themselves as supermen and lived each one for himself alone; they used violence and force against their weaker neighbors, paying no attention to laws and rules. The new generation of mankind was different. They stressed the opposite code of living. The individual did not count for himself; he counted only as part of the community, and he had to subject his own interests to those of the group. Had they confined themselves to this kind of social life, all might have been well. But they overdid it. The tremendous strength that grew out of their organization and goodwill made them proud, and their pride made them turn against G-d.

They decided to build a tower which was to reach to heaven, to make them equal to G-d, and at the same time, to make it possible for them to stay together. This symbol of their divine strength, as they thought, was to be built in the valley of the Land of Shinear.

**THEIR
PUNISHMENT:**
G-d decided to destroy their arrogance by destroying their ability to understand one another. He, therefore, confused the people by splitting them up into seventy different nations and tribes, each with a language of its own, (hence the name Babel, meaning "confusion").

THE RUINS OF BABYLON

When this happened, the project of the Tower had to be given up. The various groups migrated in different directions and settled in all parts of the world. The Tower itself was partly burned and partly swallowed by the earth.

NIMROD: But even this severe punishment did not bring the people back to the ways of G-d. During the time of Nimrod, who was the grandson of Ham, the wickedness of the people increased tremendously. Nimrod had inherited the clothes of Adam, made out of the skin of the Serpent, and he was unconquerable. All the animals of the world obeyed him and kings recognized his rule. He proclaimed himself god, and images of his face were shown all over the country. People had to serve him and bring him offerings.

It was in this age of idolatry that a new star appeared on the horizon—the only shining star in a dark sky.

TEST YOUR KNOWLEDGE

1. Place the following in the order of their creation: Man, bird, fish, lion? (pp. 1, 2)

2. What is the meaning of "Adam," "Gan Eden," "Etz Hadath,"? (pp. 2, 3)

3. Who murdered a quarter of the world's population? (p. 6)

4. Who said, "Am I my brother's keeper?" (p. 6)

5. Who committed the first manslaughter? (p. 7)

6. Who lived longer than any man on eath? (p. 9)

7. How many people entered Noah's Ark? (p. 9)

8. How old was Noah when the Flood commenced? (p. 10)

9. In what connection is the dove first mentioned in the Bible? (p. 11)

10. Who was Malkitzedek? (p. 13)

11. Name and explain the "Seven Laws" given by G-d to Noah and his children after the Flood? (p. 12)

12. What is the origin of the name "Babel? (p. 14)

13. Who was Nimrod? (p. 19)

II. THE STORY OF OUR FOREFATHERS

8. ABRAM *

ABRAM'S FAMILY: One of the most important persons at Nimrod's court in Ur of the Chaldees in Babel, or Babylonia, was Terah, the son of Nahor, a great-great grandson of Eber. Terah had three sons, Abram, Nahor, and Haran.

ABRAM'S BIRTH: The night before Abram was born, Nimrod's astrologers were gathered at Terah's house. Looking out into the night sky, they read in the constellation of the stars that the newly born child was to become the chief and the father of a mighty nation. This discovery was communicated to Nimrod, who became afraid that the new star might darken his own.

NIMROD'S ATTEMPT ON ABRAM'S LIFE: Nimrod asked Terah to bring the newly born baby to the palace to be killed. Terah tried to talk Nimrod out of it, but he couldn't. He risked his life and the lives of his whole family, and exchanged his son with a servant's child born the same day as Abram. Nimrod did not suspect the ruse, and he killed the baby with his own hands. Meanwhile, Abram was hidden in a cave.

YOUNG ABRAM RECOGNIZES G-D Abram stayed in the cave until he was ten years old. During this time he came to believe in the existence of G-d through reasoning. Abram had watched

---

* Later G-d renamed him Abraham.

the sun and the moon and the stars coming and going, each in its own time. He had noticed the sun giving way to the moon, despite its apparent divine power, and the moon giving place to the sun in the morning. And so he reasoned that there must be a Power above and beyond all the visible forces of nature, a Power Who had created them, and Who regulated and controlled them at all times. Behind the limited power of all nature, young Abram perceived the unlimited and timeless existence of G-d.

Then G-d made Himself known to Abram and taught him the right way of living. Later Abram went to the house of Noah and Shem. There he stayed many years; there he studied and learned to serve G-d.

ABRAM DESTROYS THE IDOLS: Nimrod had long forgotten the threat of the new star which his astrologers had predicted. He had rewarded Terah for his faithfulness and had given him even higher honors than before. For Terah was clever, and Nimrod took his advice in matters of state. Besides, Terah had always appeared an obedient servant with regard to the new idols Nimrod introduced in his empire. Nimrod had no reason to hold any grudge against Terah, in spite of his astrologers' predictions.

Abram had been taught the knowledge of the true G-d, and he despised the idol worship of the people around him. He therefore decided to do everything in his power to crush the belief in idol worship. He talked to all the visitors at his father's house and convinced many that their belief in idols was false and foolish. But Terah refused to listen to his son's reasoning.

One day, Abram took an axe and destroyed all his father's idols. Only the largest remained intact. When Terah saw his idols shattered and scattered all over the floor, he accused Abram. But Abram said that the largest of the idols had killed all the others in a fight over an offering brought to them. Terah exclaimed that such a thing was impossible, since idols could not quarrel or fight. Then he realized that his son tricked him into admitting that the idols made of stone and wood could not even move, and he became very angry. Forgetting that he had long ago deceived Nimrod by substituting another child for Abram, he went to the king and reported his son's irreverence towards the gods.

IN NIMROD'S HANDS: Nimrod had Abram thrown into prison and condemned to death by fire. Hundreds of people crowded to watch the son of Prince Terah burn alive for disloyalty and disrespect towards the gods. For Abram had not kept quiet when he was brought before the king. He accused Nimrod of reducing his people to the idolatrous state of the generation before the Flood. When Abram was condemned to die by fire, he exclaimed before the court that Nimrod had no power against the will of G-d. The fire could never harm him if G-d did not wish it to, for He who gave fire the strength to burn, could take it away. His courageous speech had spread all over the country, and everyone, rich and poor, young and old, was eager to find out whether Abram was right, or whether he was just a boastful dreamer.

THE MIRACLE IN THE FURNACE: Abram was thrown into the fiery furnace. But G-d was with him and the fire did not touch him. It only burned the rope which bound him.

For three whole days and nights, hundreds of people could hardly believe their eyes, seeing Abram walking in the midst of the flames, without having even a hair of his head singed. King Nimrod himself had to admit that Abram had spoken the truth and that he was a man of G-d. He asked Abram to come out of the furnace. Nimrod then gave Abram many presents and sent him back to his father's house. But Abram did not go alone. For with him went two hundred men of noble descent, amongst them, Eliezer of Damascus, who was later to become Abram's most trusted servant. They all abandoned Nimrod and his rich court to live with Abram and learn from him the knowledge of the true G-d.

Abram married Sarai.* He lived with Terah until Nimrod sent for him again, this time intending to kill him secretly. But Abram learned of this plot in time, and escaped to Noah's house, where he had lived as a young man. Terah followed him there, and together they went to Haran in *Aram Naharaim,* or Mesopotamia.

G-D'S COMMAND AND PROMISE TO ABRAM: But the people in Mesopotamia did not worship G-d. They worshipped all kinds of idols and followed the wicked ways of Nimrod and his people. G-d saw that Abram was the only one who was righteous and G-d fearing. G-d, therefore, appeared to Abram and said: "Go out of thy country, and from thy kindred, and thy father's house, unto the land that I shall show thee. And I will make of thee a great nation, and I will bless thee, and make thy name great; and be thou a blessing. And I will bless them that bless thee, and curse him that curseth thee; and in thee shall all the families of the earth be blessed."

---

* Later G-d renamed her Sarah.

ABRAM'S OBEDIENCE: Abram did as G-d told him. At the age of seventy-five years, he left Haran, accompanied by his wife Sarai, and nephew Lot, the son of his brother Haran. They wandered into the land of Canaan. Here, near the city of Shechem, in the oak groves of Moreh, G-d again appeared to Abram and said: "This land I shall give to thy children." Abram built an altar to G-d and travelled through the country to spread the knowledge of G-d wherever he went.

9. ABRAM AND LOT

ABRAM GOES TO EGYPT: While Abram was on this journey, a famine broke out in the land, and Egypt, so long known as the storehouse of the world, became the goal of Abram's wandering. Knowing the evil ways and morals of the Egyptians, Abram tried to hide his fair wife Sarai. But the custom-officers discovered her and took her into King Pharoah's palace, believing her to be Abram's sister and not his wife. At night, G-d appeared to Sarai and assured her that nothing would happen to her. And G-d smote Pharaoh and his men with plagues, and they could not touch Sarai. When they found out the reason for all the trouble that had come to them, Pharoah called Abram and rebuked him for not having revealed to him that Sarai was his wife. Then he sent Abram and Sarai away, after he had given them many gifts of cattle and servants.

THE STRIFE OF THE HERDSMEN: The famine ended, and Abram and his household, among them his nephew Lot, returned to their old place in Canaan, between Beth-El and Ay. Abram was now very rich. He had flocks, silver, and gold in abundance. Lot also had a great number of sheep and cattle. But whereas Abram's shepherds abided strictly by the rules given to them by their pious master concerning trespassing upon the property of others, Lot's shepherds were rough men who did not respect this spirit of justice. Thus there were constant arguments and strife between the herdsmen of Abram and Lot. Soon complaints reached Abram about the misbehavior of Lot's herdsmen and the strife between the shepherds. Abram therefore called Lot and said to him: "Let there be no strife, I pray thee, between me and thee, and between my herdsmen and thy herdsmen; for we are brethren. Is not the whole land before thee? Separate thyself, I pray thee, from me; if thou wilt take the left hand, then I will go to the right, or if thou take the right hand, then I will go to the left."

ABRAM AND LOT SEPARATE: Abram and Lot were standing on the height near Beth-El, and from this point they gazed over a wide extent of country. They looked down into the fruitful and blooming valley of the Jordan; it was indeed like the garden of Eden, or like the rich land of Egypt they had just left. But the people of these lovely districts "were wicked and sinners before G-d exceedingly." Lot made his choice without hesitation; and separating himself from his generous and unselfish kinsman, he journeyed eastward, and finally pitched his tent near Sodom, in the valley of the Jordan.

Abram, left alone in his encampment near Beth-El, received from G-d another of those promises so full of hope and gladness. He was bidden to lift his eyes to the north and south, the east and west; for all that land should belong to him and to his descendants forever. And great and numerous should be his offspring, for G-d pledged, "I shall make thy seed as the dust of the earth, so that if a man can number the dust of the earth, then thy seed shall also be numbered. Arise, pass through the land, in its length and in its breadth; for to thee I shall give it."

Thus commanded by G-d, Abram journed southward, till he reached the city of Kiryath Arba, later called Hebron. There he was welcomed by Aner, Eshkol and Mamre, the resident lords of the Amorites. They formed an alliance, and Abram settled down in the oak-groves of Mamre.

LOT A PRISONER OF WAR: Lot was soon to discover that his greed for wealth had nearly cost him not only his entire fortune but also his life.

On the plain of the Jordan there were five old cities, Sodom and Gomorrah, Admah, Zebaim, and Bela or Zoar. These cities had been conquered by Chedarlaomer, the powerful king of Elam, on the east of the Tigris. For twelve years these cities paid tribute to him, but then they rebelled, and regained their independence for thirteen years. The following year, however, the great king of Elam resolved upon crushing his former satellites; and with the help of three neighboring kings, he marched from his territory, confident of success. After having gained many victories in the east and south of the land, the kings descended upon the valley of the Jordan, the real object of their trip. The five cities trembled with terror at the approach of the conquerors. Yet, anxious to resist the invaders to the last, the kings of the five cities marched out at the head of their armies and met the enemy in the valley of Siddim, near the dangerous bitumen pits, which they hoped would entrap the unwary strangers. A desperate battle was fought. The four eastern kings overpowered their unfortunate opponents, and trapped the kings of Sodom and Gemorrah in the very bitumen pits which were to have become their own graves. The others fled in trembling haste towards the mountainous lands of Jericho. All their rich possessions fell into the hands of the conquerors.

Amongst the captives was Lot, Abram's nephew, who had remained in Sodom, his chosen place of residence. Abram was in the oak-groves of Mamre, when a messenger, who had escaped from the battlefield, arrived with the news that Abram's nephew was a prisoner, a slave of the great king of Elam.

THE RESCUE: Abram immediately gathered all his men, three hundred and eighteen in number, and pursued Chedarlaomer's victorious army. It was a daring act, but it proved Abram's firm belief in G-d's help and justice. Attacking by night and aided by many divine miracles, his small band of warriors defeated the overwhelmingly superior forces of Chedarlaomer. He recaptured all the loot, freed the people, and brought them back in a march of triumph, singing praises to G-d for His miraculous help wherever he went.

Laden with this wealth, and accompanied by Lot and his released fellow-captives, the conquering Abram returned towards his home. In the valley of Shaveh he was met by the king of Sodom, who came forth with Malkitzedek, the king of Salem, who, as mentioned before, was Shem, the son of Noah, and priest of G-d. In accordance with his priestly office, he brought bread and wine, which he gave to Abram, adding to this typical offering a blessing so true and simple: "Blessed be Abram of the Most High G-d, Who has delivered thy enemies into thy hand." Abram gave him a tenth of everything he had.

The king of Sodom satisfied with the liberation of his captured hosts and country by Abram, gratefully offered to him the whole of the spoil he had brought back; but Abram, unwilling to be enriched by the wealth of idol worshippers, refused everything "from a thread to a shoe-latchet"; yet he permitted his faithful allies Aner, Eshkol, and Mamre to take their due portions.

10. THE COVENANT

COUNT THE STARS: After Abram's victory over Chedarlaomer G-d appeared to Abram and promised him further protection and great reward. Abram exclaimed, "Of what avail is all my wealth if I go childless, and there be no one to carry on my work after me?"

The answer full of comfort came forthwith, that no stranger should be his heir, but his own child. To enhance the force of these words, G-d called Abram from his tent and told him to look upwards to the heavens. The next moment Abram was standing at the door of his tent, gazing upwards and listening to the Divine words: "Look now towards heaven, and number the stars, if thou be able to number them; so shall thy seed be."

Although Abram was already an old man and his wife could hardly be expected to have children, now after she had been childless for so many years, Abram believed this promise, and G-d gave him much credit for his great faith.

Again G-d appeared to him in a vision, this time not altogether of a comforting nature. "Know of a surety," said G-d, "that thy seed will be a stranger in a land that is not theirs and they will enslave them, and will afflict them —four hundred years. But that nation also which they will serve, I will judge, and afterwards they shall return hither, for the iniquity of the Amorites is not yet complete." As the voice of G-d ceased in the midst of the dense darkness, a flame descended upon the sacrifice Abram had offered up; and while the animals were consumed, G-d reappeared: "To thy seed have I given this land from the river of Egypt to the great river, the river Euphrates."

ABRAM TAKES HAGAR AS WIFE: The fame of Abram's victory and his noble character spread far and wide, and he gained the respect and admiration of everyone. Abram would have been happy indeed, but for the fact that G-d had not blessed him with an heir. He and Sarai were growing old and longed for a child. When Abram reached his eighty-fifth birthday, Sarai asked him to marry her maid Hagar.*

Abram accepted Sarai's advice and took Hagar as wife. She bore him a son, whom he called Ishmael, "G-d will hear."

THE COVENANT: When Abram was ninety-nine years old, G-d appeared unto him again and changed his name from Abram to Abraham, meaning "the father of a multitude of nations." Sarai also received the direct blessing of G-d; before she had been called Sarai, but now she should be known by the noble and proud name of Sarah, "Queen": "I shall bless her," said G-d, "and she shall be a mother of nations; kings of peoples shall be of her."

G-d then made a covenant with Abraham. According to this covenant Abraham and his future generations must follow in the path of G-d, and G-d promised them the land of Canaan and His protection and care. The command

---

* Originally a princess in Pharaoh's house Hagar preferred to be a maid in Abraham's.

for circumcision (Brith) was then given as a symbol of this covenant. Every newly born Jewish boy should be circumcised at the age of eight days. Abraham himself, despite his ripe age, and all the male members of his household, underwent that operation, and the covenant was established for all generations to come.

ABRAHAM'S GUESTS: Abraham was recovering from his operation when G-d visited him in his tent in the groves of Mamre. The day was hot and Abraham was in pain.

It was not so much the discomfort of the heat that troubled Abraham, as the thought that the blazing sun was keeping all wayfarers off the road. G-d decided that He would not deprive Abraham of the pleasure of welcoming guests and visitors. G-d sent three angels disguised as wandering Arabs to walk past the grove. Abraham saw the wandering Arabs and ran forth to meet and greet them, forgetting all his pain.

He urged them not to pass by but to rest beneath the shade of the trees, whilst he fetched water to wash their feet, and bread for refreshment. No servant was to assist in preparing the strangers' meal, but Sarah herself baked the cakes of fine flour, while Abraham hastened to the herd, choosing a young and tender calf, which was made ready without delay. Only later, when the angels announced that a year from that day Sarah would give birth to a son, did Abraham realize who his guests were; and happiness filled his heart. Sarah too, heard the message, and could hardly believe that at the age of ninety she was yet to be blessed with a child!

11. THE DESTRUCTION OF SODOM

THE WICKEDNESS OF THE SODOMITES: The angels left Abraham's tent, and two of them turned in the direction of Sodom to carry out G-d's decision to destroy that city.

The Sodomites were notorious for their wickedness. They had no consideration for the poor, nor for the passing stranger to whom they offered no hospitality; nor would they even sell him any food or water. Once they had found out that Plitith, Lot's daughter, had secretly given food to a stranger who was near starvation, and they burned her in public. Another time, when they discovered that a young girl had fed a starving beggar, they smeared honey all over her and placed her upon the city wall, so that she died from the stings of the bees attracted by the honey.

These and many other similar hideous acts of cruelty by the Sodomites and their neighbors of Gomorrah, had aroused G-d's anger, and He decided to destroy them completely.

ARAHAM PLEADS FOR SODOM: When G-d informed Abraham of his intention to destroy Sodom and Gomorrah, Abraham pleaded with G-d to save the cities for the sake of the righteous who might be living there. Only when G-d had promised him that if there were even ten righteous inhabitants in Sodom, He would save the entire city for their sake, did Abraham plead no more.

LOT'S HOSPITALITY: Lot, Abraham's nephew, could never forget completely his uncle's teachings and ways of living. Although he had been associating with the Sodomites for many years, he had not accepted their attitude towards strangers, and he did not share in their cruel treatment of the unfortunate passer-by.

Lot had been sitting at the gates of Sodom when he saw two strangers. He greeted them and invited them to his tent, although he knew full well that he risked his life by doing so. The strangers at first refused, but after Lot persuaded them, they finally agreed to follow him into his house.

The people of Sodom, having learned of the presence of strangers, surrounded Lot's house. They demanded that Lot give up the two visitors to be dealt with in the usual manner. In vain did Lot try to quiet them and persuade them to leave the strangers alone. The more he spoke to them, the more excited they became. Finally, they threatened to kill Lot and proceeded to storm the house. But the angels pulled Lot back into the house and struck the attacking mob with blindness, so that they could not force their way into Lot's house.

LOT AND HIS FAMILY ARE SAVED: Thereupon, the angels told Lot to take his entire family and leave the city immediately, for G-d had sent them to destroy Sodom. But Lot's sons-in-law were Sodomites and refused to leave their homes. Morning dawned, and the angels took Lot, his wife, and two unwed daughters, and led them out of the town, forbidding them to turn back and look at the city. As soon as Lot had reached Zoar, G-d rained brimstone and fire upon Sodom and Gomorrah. The place that had once looked like a divine garden was turned into a sea of salt. Lot's wife was too curious to obey the command of the angels. She turned around to look back at the city where they had lived so long. The punishment followed instantaneously; she was changed into a pillar of salt. Lot ultimately left Zoar, and he and his descendants inhabited the provinces of Moab and Ammon.

**THE
DEAD SEA:**
Abraham, remembering G-d's gracious promise, hastened early in the morning to the spot where he had prayed to G-d on the previous day. The blooming valley was hidden by smoke; giant furnaces rose from earth to heaven where the proud cities of the Jordan stood; and the wild flames were rapidly consuming the land. When the devastation was complete, a vast lake of salt and asphalt, or bitumen, "The Dead Sea," lay to the east of the desert of Judah.

The Dead Sea remained, and is now one of the marvels of the earth.

**ABRAHAM
IN GERAR:**
The destruction of Sodom brought fear into many hearts. Wayfarers and caravans began to shun that part of the land, and soon the roads leading to the once fertile regions of Sodom became all but deserted.

Abraham decided to move south. He left Hebron, where he had dwelt for twenty-five years and went to Gerar, in the land of the Philistines. As he had done in Egypt many years earlier, Abraham again concealed the fact that Sarah was his wife, fearing that the Philistines might want to slay him. Believing that Sarah was Abraham's sister, King Abimelech of the Philistines had her brought to the palace. But G-d smote the king and his servants with plagues, so that they would not touch her. As soon as the king found out the cause of his punishment he called Abraham and begged his forgiveness. To make up for his wrong, he gave Abraham and Sarah many gifts. Abraham prayed to G-d to cure Abimelech and his royal household, and the prayers were answered. Abimelech and his people knew that Abraham was a saintly man, and they begged him to stay in their land. Abraham, agreed, and resided in Gerar for twenty-six years.

ISAAC'S BIRTH: God's promise was fulfilled. When Abraham was one hundred years old and his wife ninety, Sarah gave birth to a son. Abraham called him Isaac and circumcised him on the eighth day, making him a party to the holy covenant G-d had established with Abraham.

ISHMAEL: As we know, Isaac was not Abraham's first-born, for Hagar had borne him Ishmael thirteen years earlier. But Ishmael had not grown up as his father had hoped. He was inclined towards many things Abraham considered wicked. Ishmael even prayed to idols when he believed himself unobserved.

Sarah observed him and realized that he would have a bad influence upon the young Isaac. She therefore implored Abraham to send Ishmael away. Abraham understood the motive of his wife's request, but he feared to send his son away to a place where he might become even worse. However, G-d told Abraham to do as Sarah had requested, and Abraham then sent Hagar and Ishmael away, providing them with water and food for the journey.

THE MIRACLE: Hagar and Ishmael lost their way in the wilderness of Beer Sheba and soon ran out of water. Hagar could not watch the boy's suffering and put him in the shade of a bush, while she sat some distance away and cried. An angel then called to Hagar and assured her that G-d had seen the suffering of her boy. He would live and become the father of a mighty nation. And suddenly, Hagar saw a spring nearby.

Hagar and Ishmael were saved from death and continued their journey. G-d blessed the boy, for he was Abraham's son. Ishmael grew up into a strong man. He lived on the outskirts of the desert and became a great archer. Ishmael lived his life in his own way. He married and had many children. His children multiplied and became known under the name of Ishmaelites, or Arabs, the people of the desert.

12. THE GREAT TEST

G-D'S STRANGE COMMAND: Peace and harmony had returned to Abraham's house, after Ishmael and his mother had left. But Abraham was not to find complete peace. Once more his faith was to be tested severely.

Under stress of tribulation Abraham had proved unshaken in his faith in G-d. Would his faith be just as strong in the midst of blissfulness? G-d now put Abraham's sincerity and obedience to the greatest possible test. Appearing to Abraham suddenly, G-d said to him, "Take now thy son, thine only son, whom thou lovest, Isaac, and get thee into the land of Moriah; and bring him up there as a burnt-offering upon one of the mountains which I will tell thee of."

Abraham did not plead with G-d for his son. He did not ask how this command could be reconciled with the promise that Isaac was to become the father of a large nation that was to bear G-d's name. G-d commanded, and Abraham hastened to obey.

FATHER AND SON TOGETHER: Abraham rose early in the morning, saddled his ass with his own hands and prepared wood for the fire; then he took two servants and his son Isaac and started on the trip to Moriah. Isaac, then already a fully grown man of thirty-seven, soon realized for what purpose he was being taken on this trip.

Thus father and son were firm in their decision to fulfill G-d's command. Many an obstacle was put in their way to make it difficult for them to go through with the test. However, with firm hearts and solemn determination, Abraham and Isaac continued on their way until they reached Mount Moriah on the third day. Here G-d showed Abraham the place where he was to build the altar and bind Isaac on it. Abraham and Isaac ascended to the place G-d had designated.

THE AKEDAH: Having prepared the altar, upon which he bound his beloved son, Abraham lifted the knife to sacrifice Isaac. At that moment an angel called unto him to halt and do no harm to his son, for this was only a test and Abraham had proved his loyalty to G-d. Full of gratitude and holy inspiration, Abraham looked around and saw a ram that had been caught in a thicket by his horns. Abraham took the ram and offered it, instead of Isaac, to G-d.

ABRAHAM'S REWARD: And the angel of G-d called unto Abraham a second time out of heaven and said, " 'By Myself have I sworn,' saith G-d, 'because thou hast done this thing, and hast not withheld thy son, thine only son, that I will bless thee, and I will multiply thy seed as the stars of the heaven, and as the sand which is upon the sea-shore; and thy seed shall possess the gate of his enemies; and in thy seed shall all

nations of the earth be blessed; because thou hast hearkened
to My voice.' "

**ABRAHAM AND ISAAC
RETURN:**
Full of happiness and
solemn joy at the miracu-
lous ending of their trip,
Abraham and Isaac descended from the mountain and returned to the place where they had left their servants.
As fast as they could, they returned home to Sarah. Abraham feared that somehow Sarah might have guessed the
real purpose of the journey, and he was therefore anxious
to return home with his beloved son Isaac safe and sound.

**SARAH'S
DEATH:**
News of Isaac's safe return reached Sarah
before his arrival, and her troubled heart
could not stand the shock. Sarah died from
the shock of happiness that overwhelmed her. She was
one hundred and twenty-seven years old.

Abraham mourned deeply over the loss of his wife,
and with him mourned the entire country. He bought
the Cave of Machpelah, near Hebron, where Adam and
Eve had been buried, and there he laid his wife Sarah to
rest.

13. ISAAC'S MARRIAGE

**ELIEZER'S
MISSION:**
For three years Sarah's tent remained
vacant. Gloom and loneliness prevailed
where light and life had been pulsing before,
as long as Sarah had lived.

Abraham was eager to have Isaac marry a woman
of the character and stature of Sarah. Isaac himself was
completely immersed in the study and in the service of
G-d. It was obvious to Abraham that he could not find a

THE CAVE OF MACHPELAH

suitable girl for his son among the Canaanite neighbors. Their upbringing and way of life were too different from Abraham's and Isaac's, and none of them could ever become his son's companion for life, and the true heiress of Sarah.

Abraham, therefore, decided to look for a daughter-in-law among the children of his brother Nahor. He called his trusted servant Eliezer, who had been in charge of Abraham's household affairs ever since he had left Nimrod's court. Abraham made Eliezer promise on oath that he would go to Nahor in Mesopotamia to find a wife for Isaac.

Taking ten camels, laden with the best of his master's treasures, Eliezer left for Mesopotamia on his sacred mission.

ELIEZER'S PRAYER: Eliezer arrived safely and stopped his camels near a well outside the city. It was evening, the time when the women of the city came to draw water, and Eliezer prayed: "O Lord, the G-d of my master Abraham, send me I pray Thee, good speed this day, and show kindness unto my master Abraham. Behold, I stand by the fountain of water; and the daughters of the men of the city come out to draw water. So let it come to pass, that the damsel to whom I shall say: 'Let down thy pitcher, I pray thee, that I may drink,' and she shall say: 'Drink, and I will give thy camels drink also,' let the same be she whom Thou hast appointed for Thy servant, for Isaac; and thereby I shall know that Thou hast shown kindness unto my master."

REBEKAH AT THE WELL: Hardly had Eliezer concluded his prayer, when he saw Rebekah, the daughter of Abraham's nephew Bethuel, approaching. She was beautiful, and Eliezer was impressed by her gracious behavior. She carried a pitcher on her shoulder, stepped down to the well, and filled it. When she came up again, Eliezer asked to be permitted to drink from her pitcher. Rebekah answered, "Drink my lord." When he had quenched his thirst, she said: "For your camels I will also draw water until they have had enough." With these words she emptied her pitcher into the trough, and filled it time and again until all the camels had drunk their fill. Eliezer felt sure that this was the girl he was looking for. Without even asking her name, he gave her a golden ring and two bracelets, and only then asked her who she was. When Rebekah answered that she was the granddaughter of Nahor, Abraham's brother, Eliezer bowed before G-d and thanked Him for having helped him find the woman Abraham was looking for to be Isaac's wife.

Rebekah hurried home to tell her people about her meeting with Eliezer. Her brother Laban ran out to the well to welcome Eliezer into the house. Soon Abraham's servant told Bethuel and his family about his mission and how G-d had miraculously helped him to find Rebekah, their daughter, to be the worthy wife of his master's son Isaac. Laban and Bethuel replied that since G-d Himself favored this match, they would not hinder it, and that he could take Rebekah with him to his master's son Isaac.

ISAAC MARRIES REBEKAH: The next morning when Eliezer asked permission to leave for home with the girl, her people were reluctant to let her go immediately. They suggested that she stay for at least another year to prepare for her wedding. Finally, however, the choice was left to Rebekah, and she eagerly gave her consent to leave immediately. Rebekah had never relished her surroundings and environment and was happy to become a member of the house of Abraham, whose fame was world-wide.

Isaac had gone out in the fields to pray one evening, when Eliezer's caravan returned. Eliezer related his adventures, and Abraham and Isaac were very thankful to G-d. Isaac's marriage to Rebekah was celebrated without delay, and Rebekah occupied the tent that had once belonged to Sarah. Once again Abraham's house was fiilled with happiness, for Rebekah proved to be a worthy successor to Sarah.

14. JACOB AND ESAU

BIRTH OF THE TWINS: Twenty years had passed since Isaac's and Rebekah's marriage, but as yet, they had not been blessed with children. Finally, G-d answered Isaac's prayers, and Rebekah gave birth to twins. The first child to be born was covered with hair like a fully grown person. His parents called him Esau (from the Hebrew word "osso"—finish). The second child followed Esau, holding on to his brother's heel, and Isaac called him Jacob (*Yaakov, "One that takes by the heel"*).

JACOB AND ESAU GROW UP: Although the children were twins and grew up together, they displayed a difference in character. Jacob spent all his time at home, engaged in study with his father and grandfather Abraham. Esau, however, resorted to countless tricks to avoid studying, and spent most of his time in the fields. He enjoyed hunting and killing, and was often absent from his home for many days.

ABRAHAM'S DEATH: Abraham lived to a ripe and happy old age, and died at the age of one hundred and seventy-five. His sons, Isaac and Ishmael, buried him in the Cave of Machpelah.

ESAU KILLS NIMROD: On the day of Abraham's death, Esau had been out in the fields as usual. He had lost his way and was trying to find his way back, when King Nimrod arrived with two servants. Esau hid behind a rock, and when Nimrod was left unguarded, he killed him and fought the two servants who rushed to the aid of their master. Esau escaped with King Nimrod's clothes. These were Adam's garments which later became the property of Noah; Noah's son Ham, who was Nimrod's grandfather, had subsequently become their owner, and finally Nimrod had acquired them. These divine clothes had made Nimrod a powerful and skillful hunter and a mighty ruler over all other kings. Now Esau had come into possession of the most valuable and cherished property a hunter could desire.

JACOB BUYS THE BIRTHRIGHT: The birthright was a sacred privilege enjoyed by the first-born son. This privilege made the first-born the real heir and successor to his father, as the head of the family. Isaac's first-born son was to be devoted to the service of G-d and to the sacred traditions of the family. But in the case of Esau, it soon became apparent that he was not the one to fulfill this sacred duty. Esau did not wish to shoulder this responsibility, preferring a gay and carefree life as a hunter and man of the fields. Jacob, on the other hand, seemed the ideal heir and successor. The day that Esau returned from that fateful hunting trip, his clothes still covered with the spatter of mud and blood, Jacob scolded him for neglecting his holy duty as first-born. Esau, however, derided Jacob and spoke very mockingly of the birthright. Jacob was shocked to hear such abuse of, and disrespect towards, the sacred privilege of the first-born, and proposed to buy the birthright from

Esau who willingly agreed to make the deal. Thus Jacob came into the possession of something he cherished more than all the treasures of the world.

ISAAC GOES TO PHILISTINA: After Abraham's death, famine again swept over the land of Canaan. Isaac wanted to follow the example of his father Abraham and go to Egypt. However, G-d ordered him never to leave the land that had been promised to his father and to him, and Isaac travelled down only to the land of the Philistines. Isaac took the same precaution his father had taken when he sojourned among the Philistines. He said that Rebekah was not his wife, but his sister. King Abimelech desired to marry Rebekah, for she was the fairest woman he had ever seen. But when he found out that Rebekah was really Isaac's wife, he was afraid to touch her or Isaac. When Isaac grew very prosperous, the Philistines became envious and requested him to leave. Isaac went to Beer Sheba, where his father Abraham had dwelt. Soon after, Abimelech paid Isaac a friendly visit, desiring to make up for his former unfriendly act. Abimelech asked Isaac to make a treaty of peace with him. This Isaac did, and Abimelech returned to his land.

15. JACOB RECEIVES ISAAC'S BLESSING

ESAU'S EVIL WAYS: Although Jacob had gone to the academy of Shem and Eber to study the teachings of G-d, Esau refused to do anything of the sort. He led his life in his own way, and became more estranged from his father's teachings. Yet, he honored his father and tried to appear an obedient and loving son, ready to comply with his father's every wish, as long as it did not involve him in studying and learning. Isaac could not and did not see Esau's G-dless behavior, for his eyes were dim with age, and he was confined to his tent.

Rebekah, however, saw everything. She observed the quiet and pleasing ways of Jacob, and watched with alarm the true nature of her first-born son Esau. For her there could be no doubt as to which of her children had chosen the right way.

After the death of Shem, Jacob returned to his father's house, and Esau, too, came home from Seir. Isaac had grown old and weak and felt that the time had come for him to give his sons his last blessings.

Still believing that he could entrust Esau with the task of carrying on Abraham's tradition, Isaac told Esau to hunt some venison, prepare a meal for him, and receive his blessings. Gladly, Esau took his bow and quiver and went out into the field.

REBEKAH'S RUSE: Rebekah had heard what her husband told Esau, and in a moment her resolve was taken. Esau should not receive the blessing which, as she believed, belonged even from his birth to her younger and wiser son. She went to Jacob, and hastily related to him what she had heard, and then she suggested to him that he prepare some meat and bring it to his father in the disguise of his brother Esau. Jacob was loath to deceive his father, even though he knew his mother was right. But Rebekah ordered him to do as she said, taking full responsibility for the act.

Jacob did not dare to refuse his mother, and so he fetched two tender kids from the flock, and Rebekah prepared them so that they tasted like venison. Then she dressed her younger son in the festive garments of Esau, and to render the resemblance perfect, she covered his smooth neck and hands with the skins of the kids. She then put the meal into his hands and sent him to his father.

THE BLESSING: Isaac wondered at his son's early return, and at his soft-spoken and pious address. Feeling Jacob's arms and neck, Isaac exclaimed: "The voice is the voice of Jacob, but the hands are the hands of Esau!" Isaac ate of the meat Jacob brought him. Then he blessed his son with the words: "And may G-d give thee of the dew of heaven and of the fatness of the earth, and plenty of corn and wine. Let peoples serve thee and nations bow down to thee. Be lord over thy brethren, and let thy mother's children bow down to thee. Cursed be every one that curseth thee, and blessed be every one that blesseth thee!"

ESAU RETURNS: Hardly had Jacob left Isaac, when Esau returned from the hunt. He prepared the venison and brought it to his father. He soon learned what had happened in the meantime, and cried with anger and disappointment. Isaac blessed him too, giving him the right to throw off the yoke of his brother whenever his brother strayed from the path of G-d. But Esau hated Jacob, and Jacob evaded the ire of his brother by returning to Eber to study under his care.

16. JACOB'S FLIGHT

REBEKAH SENDS JACOB TO HARAN: During Jacob's absence, Esau's hatred had died down. But as soon as Jacob returned from Eber, his old grudge flared up, and day and night he brooded over a scheme to kill Jacob. Yet, he feared his father too much to cause him such grief, and he decided to postpone his revenge until after Isaac's death.

But Rebekah observed Esau and understood that his gloomy scheming boded ill for Jacob. She, therefore, spoke to Isaac and asked him to send Jacob to her brother Laban in Haran for some time, to seek out a wife for himself from Laban's daughters, Jacob's cousins. Isaac readily consented, recommended his son to take a wife from the daughters of Laban, and dismissed him with a fervent and affectionate benediction: "And may G-d the Almighty bless thee, and make thee fruitful, and multiply thee, that thou mayest inherit the land of thy sojourn, which G-d gave to Abraham."

JACOB AND ELIPHAZ: With his father's blessings still ringing in his ears, Jacob left Beer Sheba, and proceeded on his way to his uncle Laban in Padan Aram. Esau soon found out that his brother had left the house. He immediately sent his oldest son Eliphaz with ten armed men to pursue and kill Jacob. But Eliphaz, instead of murdering his uncle, agreed to take all Jacob's possessions, and let Jacob continue on his way.

JACOB'S DREAM: The day waned, and night found the wanderer in an open field before the town of Luz, still within the territory of Canaan. Weary from his journey, he took stones for his pillow and lay down to rest; with the earth for his couch, and the bright starlit heavens for his canopy, he fell asleep. And in his rest he was favored by a marvellous dream. A vast ladder seemed to rise beside him, the foot of which rested upon the earth, and the top of which reached to heaven. Up and down this ladder ascended and descended the angels of G-d. From above came the voice of G-d, as it had come to

THE JORDAN ABOVE JERICHO

Abraham and Isaac, promising him strength: "I am the Lord, the G-d of Abraham, thy father and the G-d of Isaac: the land whereon thou liest, to thee shall I give it, and to thy seed; and thy seed shall be as the dust of the earth, and thou shalt spread to the west and to the east, and to the north and to the south; and in thee and thy seed shall all the families of the earth be blessed. And behold I am with thee, and I shall guard thee wherever thou goest, and shall bring thee back into this land; for I shall not leave thee until I have done that of which I have spoken to thee."

When Jacob awoke out of his sleep, he exclaimed, "Surely the Lord is in this place, and I knew it not"; and he was afraid, and said, "How awful is this place! This is none other but the house of G-d, and this is the gate of heaven."

JACOB'S VOW: Jacob rose early in the morning. He took the stone that had served him as a pillow and set it up in memory of this holy vision, and called the place—"Beth-El," the house of G-d. Then he made a vow that if G-d would be with him and return him safely to his father's house, he would erect a house of G-d where he had set up the stone, and that he would give a tenth of everything he owned to G-d.

JACOB'S ARRIVAL IN HARAN: Jacob continued his trip eastward. It was afternoon when he reached the outskirts of Haran. He found shepherds resting near a well, watching their flocks. Jacob greeted them and asked them about the town and his uncle Laban. Just then, Rachel, Laban's daughter, arrived with her father's herds. Jacob inquired why the shepherds did not water their flocks while it was still day. He was told that only the concerted efforts of all the shepherds

could remove the rock that covered the mouth of the well.
Hearing this, Jacob walked over to the well and single-
handed rolled the stone from its place. Then he watered
the herds of his uncle. Rachel, who with all the others
had watched this astonishing feat of Jacob's strength, was
overjoyed to hear that this outstanding visitor was none
other than her own cousin, the son of her father's sister.
She hurried home to tell her father about Jacob's arrival,
and Laban went out to the well to greet his nephew and
welcome him into his home.

17. JACOB AT LABAN'S

**THE PRICE OF
A WIFE:**
Jacob had spent a month in Laban's
house, tending his uncle's sheep. Laban,
very much satisfied with his nephew's
excellent service, and aware of the blessing that his
nephew's arrival seemed to have brought to his house,
wanted to make sure that he would not lose him too soon.
He therefore said to him: "You shall not serve me for
nothing because you are my relative. Tell me, what shall
be your reward?" Jacob replied that he was willing to
serve Laban seven years for the hand of his younger
daughter Rachel. Laban was satisfied with this proposi-
tion, for he could hardly find a better son-in-law, and it
had always been his wish that his daughters should be
married to his sister's sons.

Jacob served him seven years faithfully, giving up
sleep and rest in tender care of his uncle's flocks. And
G-d's blessing was with him.

When the day arrived on which Rachel was to be
wedded to him, Laban substituted Leah, his older daughter.
Having foreseen such a possibility, Jacob had arranged

with Rachel a series of signals by which she was to make her identity known to him when she was a heavily veiled bride. The good and self-effacing Rachel, however, wishing to spare her sister embarassment and shame, revealed the secret code to Leah, and Jacob did not discover the ruse until it was too late. When Jacob, discovering that his uncle had tricked him, demanded an explanation, Laban told him that it was not the custom of the land to marry off the younger daughter before the older one. If Jacob wished to get Rachel as his wife, he would have to serve him another seven years. There was nothing left for Jacob but to agree to do so, and he served Laban for an additional period for seven years.

JACOB'S CHILDREN: In addition to Leah and Rachel, Jacob married Silpa and Bilha, two members of Laban's household. Leah bore him seven children: Reuben, Simeon, Levi, Judah, Issachar, Zebulun, and a girl, Dinah. Rachel, who was childless till the seventh year of their marriage, finally was blessed with a son, Joseph, and shortly before her death with another boy, called Benjamin. Jacob's two other wives also bore him children; Bilha gave him Dan and Naphtali, and Silpa, Gad and Asher. The twelve sons of Jacob were to become the progenitors of the twelve tribes of Israel.

JACOB'S WEALTH: After the birth of Joseph, Jacob planned to return to Canaan. During the fourteen years he had lived with his kinsman, the house of the latter had been blessed and had prospered, and his wealth and possessions had increased. Jacob now felt that the time had come for him to return to Beer Sheba; he was ninety-one years of age and still an exile and a servant. So he entreated Laban to let him depart; but

Laban could not bear the thought of losing him, knowing of the divine blessing that rested on everything Jacob touched. Therefore, he promised him part of his flocks as reward for his services, so that Jacob could make his own fortune. Jacob stayed on for an additional six years. However, Laban tried all kinds of tricks and ruses to cheat Jacob out of the payment due him by their agreement. But G-d blessed Jacob, and his flocks multiplied rapidly, until he became a rich man. In fact, Jacob's flocks thrived so well that he became the object of much admiration all over the country, and sheep breeders from far and wide came to deal with Jacob. Thus his wealth was increased many times, and his household was augmented with many servants and slaves.

18. JACOB RETURNS TO CANAAN

JACOB LEAVES LABAN: Laban's sons envied Jacob because of his good luck and wealth, and Laban too, seeing all his evil plans to deprive Jacob of the just reward for his services foiled, became unfriendly towards his son-in-law.

Then G-d spoke to Jacob: "Return to the land of thy fathers, and I shall be with thee." Jacob asked his wives to come out to the field where he was with his herds, and said to them: "You know that I have served your father with all my strength. Yet he has deceived me so often and changed my wages ten times. But G-d did not permit him to do me evil. Now G-d has ordered me to return to the land of my birth." Rachel and Leah replied: "Whatever G-d told you to do, do!"

Assured of his wives' approval, Jacob prepared everything necessary for the long and difficult journey. He did not reveal his intentions to Laban, knowing that his uncle would not let him go. One day, when Laban was away, Jacob left for Canaan with his wives, children, and everything that belonged to him. As soon as Laban heard of Jacob's secret departure, he gathered his men and pursued him.

Catching up with Jacob on the border of the Land of Canaan, Laban planned to attack his son-in-law the following morning. However, that night Laban had a strange dream in which G-d warned him not to do any harm to Jacob. On the following morning, Laban met Jacob and complained of his secret flight, which had not given him an opportunity to bid farewell to his daughters and grandchildren. But Jacob answered that the bad treatment he had been given at Laban's house made him afraid that Laban would take his daughters away from him. Said he: "These twenty years have I been with thee; thy ewes and thy she-goats have not cast their young, and the rams of thy flock have I not eaten. That which was torn of beasts I brought not unto thee; I bore the loss of it; of my hand didst thou require it, whether stolen by day or stolen by night. Thus I was: in the day the drought consumed me, and the frost by night; and my sleep fled from mine eyes. These twenty years have I been in thy house: I served thee fourteen years for thy two daughters, and six years for some of thy flock, and thou hast changed my wages ten times. Exept the G-d of my father, the G-d of Abraham and the Fear of Isaac, had been on my side, surely now hadst thou sent me away empty. G-d hath seen mine affliction and the labor of my hands, and gave judgment yesternight."

Finally, Laban made a covenant with Jacob, and then kissed his daughters and grandchildren, blessed them, and returned home. Jacob, too, continued his trip, and the angels of G-d were with him wherever he went.

LABAN INSTIGATES ESAU TO MAKE WAR ON HIS BROTHER: As soon as Laban had departed from Jacob, he sent his son Beor to Esau, in the hills of Seir, to inform him about the great wealth Jacob had amassed during the years of service in his, Laban's, house. "Now would be the right time for you to take revenge for the injustice Jacob had done to you, and to take away all of Jacob's possessions," Laban told him. Esau did not need any more coaxing to reawaken his old hatred and whet his appetite for Jacob's wealth. He gathered four hundred able-bodied and well-trained and equipped men and moved against Jacob, whose caravan by that time had reached the river Yabok.

JACOB'S STRATEGY: Jacob heard of Esau's approaching army and sent messengers of peace and good will to his brother. He asked him to forget the old grievances since Isaac's blessings apparently had been without effect. He had experienced great hardship during these twenty years, whereas Esau was a great chieftain.

The messengers returned with disappointment. They had failed in their mission, and reported that Esau with four hundred men seemed to be in the mood to fight and to kill.

There was nothing left for Jacob to do but to prepare for the battle against his brother. He divided his camp into two, so that the one would be able to escape if the other group were defeated. And then, feeling that safety and deliverance were in the hands of G-d alone, he prayed to G-d that He be with him to help him in this uneven fight against the troops of Esau.

But, although preparing for the fight, Jacob did not abandon hope for a friendly settlement with his brother. He sent groups of servants, each bearing rich presents, to meet Esau on the way and to try thus to arouse his benevolence. At the same time he ardently prayed to G-d to turn Esau's wrath into a feeling of brotherhood.

JACOB WRESTLES WITH AN ANGEL: Crossing back to the other bank of the river to make sure he had forgotten nothing, Jacob came face to face with an angel who began to wrestle with him. It was Esau's guardian angel, who tried to defeat Jacob and have him at his mercy. But try as he might, the angel could not overcome Jacob. Nor could he shake off Jacob's firm grip. All the angel succeeded in doing was to dislocate Jacob's thigh. Morning broke, and Jacob still held on to his opponent. The angel said: "Let me go, for the day breaketh." Jacob replied: "I will not let thee go, except thou bless me." And the angel said unto him: "What is thy name?" And he said: "Jacob." And the angel said: "Thy name shall be called no more Jacob, but Israel; for thou hast striven with an angel of G-d and with men, and hast prevailed." And the angel blessed him there.

JACOB'S RECONCILATION WITH ESAU: Soon Esau arrived with his men. He had been duly impressed by the rich presents Jacob had offered him, and he abandoned his evil intentions. When Jacob, followed by his wives and children, went out to meet him, Esau embraced him and kissed him, and both cried with emotion. At first Esau refused to accept the riches which Jacob had offered him. Finally, however, he accepted them and returned to Seir.

JACOB'S ARRIVAL IN CANAAN: Jacob continued on his way to Canaan. In Beth-El he erected an altar at the place where G-d had appeared to him when he fled from Esau. Again, G-d appeared to him there, blessed him, and said: "The land I promised to Abraham and Isaac, I shall give to thee and thy children."

RACHEL'S DEATH: On the way from Beth-El to Beth-Lechem Rachel died after she had given birth to Benjamin. Jacob wanted to take her along and bury her in the Cave of Machpelah, but G-d ordered him to bury her by the wayside, on the heights of Beth-Lechem. She was to rest there, so that many years later, when her children were led into exile by the Babylonians, they would find solace and courage at her grave, knowing that Mother Rachel was imploring G-d for them.

19. JACOB IN CANAAN

THE DESTRUCTION OF SHECHEM: Jacob bought a plot of land from the people of Shechem and lived there for some time.

One day his daughter Dinah went to attend a festival of the women of Shechem. The son of Hamor, the king of Shechem, saw her and fell in love with her. He kidnapped her and forced her to stay and live with him. Jacob and his sons were horrified and humiliated by this outrage, and they were determined to avenge their sister's dishonor. They knew that even according to the laws of Shechem, this outrage was a crime punishable with death, and that the entire population of Shechem had had a share in the crime. Simeon and Levi fell upon Shechem and slew all the men, including Hamor and his son Shechem.

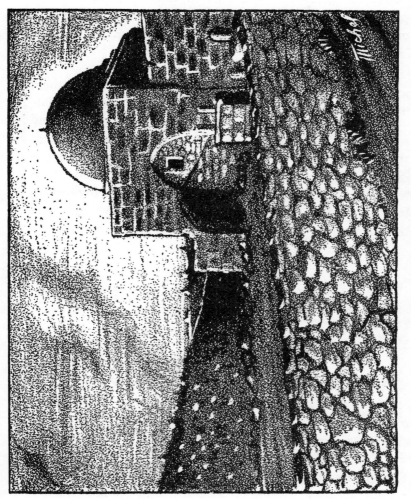

THE TOMB OF RACHEL

Jacob rebuked his sons for this action. Soon a large army of Canaanites gathered to fight Jacob and his sons. But Jacob and his father Isaac prayed to G-d, and the Canaanite kings became frightened and resolved to return to their cities without a fight.

THE WAR AGAINST THE SEVEN KINGS: Jacob moved to Hebron where his father Isaac lived. There he resided many years. Then he returned to Shechem because the land was best suited for his large flocks. Again the kings of Canaan united to destroy the children of Israel. But with the help of G-d, and under the heroic leadership of Judah, the small army, composed of Jacob's sons and servants, defeated the seven kings who had united against them. The rest of the Canaanite kings were now so afraid of Jacob's sons, that they preferred to make peace with them.

Jacob returned to Hebron, but his sons stayed with the herds near Shechem.

Isaac died at the age of one hundred and eighty, and his sons Jacob and Esau laid him to rest in the Cave of Machpelah. Esau took all the wealth and movable possessions of his father and settled in Seir, while Jacob inherited the land of Canaan, as G-d had promised.

TEST YOUR KNOWLEDGE

1. Where was Abraham born? (p. 19)

2. Relate one episode in Abraham's early childhood? (pp. 19-22)

3. What was G-d's first call to Abraham? (p. 22)

4. Can you trace Abraham's wanderings? (pp. 22, 23, 25, 32; see also map)

5. Who were Lot, Mamre, Chedarlaomer? (pp. 23, 25, 26)

6. What do you know about the origin of the Dead Sea? (p. 32)

7. How old were Abraham and Sarah when Isaac was born? (p. 33)

8. Who was Hagar? (pp. 28, 33)

9. What was Abraham's greatest test? (p. 34)

10. Who were Ishmael, Eliezer, Laban? (pp. 33, 39, 40)

11. How old was Abraham when he died? (p. 41)

12. Relate some episodes in Abraham's life showing his a) belief in one G-d, b) hospitality, c) love of peace, d) unconditional obedience to G-d, e) faith in G-d's promise.

13. Why were Jacob and Esau called by these names? (p. 41)

14. In what land did Isaac have an experience similar to his father's? (p. 43)

15. Can you complete the sentence, "The voice is the voice of Jacob and — — — "? (p. 45)

16. Who said, " . . . and this is the gate of heaven," and to what place did he refer? (p. 49)

17. How many years did Jacob spend in Haran? (pp. 51, 52)

18. What was Jacob's strategy in his reconciliation with Esau? (pp. 54, 55)

19. Where did Jacob spend his last years? (p. 59)

20. Were Jacob and Rachel buried in the same place? (pp. 56, 59)

III. JOSEPH AND HIS BROTHERS

20. JOSEPH

JACOB'S LOVE FOR JOSEPH: Jacob loved his second youngest son Joseph very dearly. Even as a young boy, Joseph had shown his great mental gifts and his piety. Since Joseph had also inherited the exquisite beauty of his mother Rachel, it is not surprising that he was his father's favorite son. Jacob spent much time teaching Joseph everything he had learned from his father and grandfather, and at the academy of Shem and Eber. And Joseph grew up to be very wise and learned. The brothers were jealous of the special favors which their father bestowed upon young Joseph. With misgivings, they viewed Joseph's company when he joined them at the age of seventeen to become a shepherd like his brothers.

JOSEPH DREAMS: Thus the relationship between Joseph and his brothers became strained. This strained relationship was brought to a climax when Joseph began to tell about his dreams which, by their very nature, affirmed his brothers' fears that he aspired to rule over them. Once Joseph told them that he had dreamed he had been binding sheaves in the field, together with them, and that their sheaves had suddenly bowed before his own. On another occasion, Joseph told his brothers of having a dream in which the sun and the moon and eleven stars had paid their respects to him.

Jacob warned Joseph against telling such dreams to his brothers, and bade his sons to disregard these dreams, for he did not wish to see strife among them. In his heart, however, he knew that there was truth in Joseph's dreams, and that Joseph was destined to become a great and powerful ruler.

JOSEPH SOLD: One day Joseph was staying home with his father, while his brothers were with the flocks near Shechem. For a long time Jacob had had no news from his sons. Worried over their fate, he sent Joseph to find them and bring word from them. Wandering all over the fields in search of his brothers, Joseph met a man who told him that they had moved in the direction of Dothan. Joseph followed them and, indeed, found them there. From afar, Joseph's brothers saw him approach. They could not mistake his coat of many colors that their father had given him, and their jealousy was aroused. They threw him into a nearby pit. Reuben had planned to take him out eventually, and return him to his father, unharmed. In the meantime, Reuben went off to wait on his father. But when he returned to the pit, Joseph was not there, for his brothers had sold him to a passing caravan of Ishmaelite merchants.

JACOB MOURNS THE LOSS OF JOSEPH: Joseph's brothers soon repented of their action. Unable to tell Jacob the truth, they slaughtered a goat and dipped Joseph's coat, which they had taken from him, into the blood. Then they sent the blood-stained garment to their father, telling him that they had found it. Jacob recognized the special garb he had made for Joseph, and thought that his favorite son had been torn to pieces by a wild animal. For many years Jacob mourned the loss of Joseph and refused to be consoled.

21. JOSEPH IN EGYPT

**IN THE SERVICE
OF POTIPHAR:**
The Ishmaelite merchants sold Joseph to a caravan of Midianites, who brought him to Egypt. There they sold him to Potiphar, who was the chief officer of King Pharaoh's guard. Joseph's extraordinary beauty, wisdom, and fine manners attracted the attention of his master. Potiphar recognized the unusual abilities of Joseph and knew that he was no common slave. He elevated him above all other servants, and soon put him in charge of the entire household. Potiphar's house throve under Joseph's able care and loyal management, for G-d was with Joseph and blessed with success everything he did.

**JOSEPH FALSELY
ACCUSED:**
In his position as supervisor of the house, Joseph could not help coming in contact with the mistress of the house and her friends. They were greatly attracted by his unusual beauty and charm.

One day, on the Feast of the Rising Nile, Joseph remained alone in the house, while the entire household turned out to attend services at the Egyptian temples. Zelicha, Potiphar's wife, also had stayed home, for she knew that Joseph would be home, since he never attended Egyptian worship. She hoped that she would have a whole day to spend in Joseph's company. But she did not know Joseph. All her promises could not tempt him to stay with her. Joseph saw his aged father before his eyes, and he could not betray the faith his father had in him. Potiphar's wife was so wicked a woman that Joseph, indignant at her conduct, escaped at last from the house of his master, leaving his cloak behind him in his hasty flight. Potiphar, returning to his house, was met by his infuriated wife who, holding the garment in her hand, greeted him with a tale against his favorite servant, accusing him of making improper advances to her.

**JOSEPH THROWN
INTO PRISON:**

Although Potiphar knew that Joseph was above suspicion and could never be guilty of such a crime, he had to uphold the honor of his wife. He had Joseph tortured and thrown into prison. There, too, however, G-d was with Joseph, and after a short while he gained the confidence of the keeper of the prison and was put in charge of the other prisoners.

**JOSEPH,
THE INTERPRETER
OF DREAMS:**

Soon thereafter, the Chief Butler and Chief Baker of King Pharaoh displeased their king by negligence in their services. Pharaoh had them thrown into the prison where Joseph was held captive. In his capacity as the prisoner-in-charge, Joseph became good friends with the two courtiers, and they spent many hours together in conversation.

One morning Joseph entered their dungeon and found them gloomy and miserable. Inquiring as to the cause of their grief, he was told that they had dreamed during the night and that there was nobody who could interpret their dreams. Joseph told them that since the meaning of dreams was in G-d's hands, they might relate their dreams to him, and, with G-d's help, perhaps he might be able to interpret them.

The Chief Butler then related his dream: "In my dream, behold, a vine was before me; and in the vine were three branches; and as it was budding, its blossoms shot forth, and the clusters thereof brought forth ripe grapes; and Pharaoh's cup was in my hand; and I took the grapes, and pressed them into Pharaoh's cup, and I gave the cup into his hand."

Joseph gave him the following interpretation: "The three branches are three days; within three days shall Pharaoh lift up thy head, and restore thee unto thine office; and thou shalt give Pharaoh's cup into his hand, after the former manner when thou wast his butler." Thinking of himself and his future, Joseph added a personal request that the Chief Butler, when back in the palace, should kindly remember him to the king, so that he too might be released from his undeserved imprisonment.

The Chief of the Bakers saw that Joseph had well interpreted the Chief Butler's dream, and he ventured to tell his dream too. He said: "I also saw in my dream, and behold, three baskets of wheat bread were on my head; and in the uppermost basket there was all manner of baked foods for Pharaoh; and the birds ate them out of the basket upon my head."

Joseph interpreted this dream to mean that in three days Pharaoh would have the Chief Baker hanged on the gallows and that the birds would pick off his flesh.

Joseph's interpretations proved right. Three days later was King Pharaoh's birthday. He reviewed the cases of the Chief Butler and Chief Baker. The former was restored to his position, but the Chief Baker was hanged. Happy, but ungrateful to Joseph, the Chief Butler forgot Joseph in the dungeon.

22. JOSEPH—VICEROY OF EGYPT

PHARAOH'S DREAMS: It was two years after Joseph had interpreted the dreams of the Chief Butler and Chief Baker, that King Pharaoh had a strange dream one night. At first he saw seven beautiful fat cows coming out of the Nile to graze on the meadow. After them seven ugly and lean cows climbed out of the water and swallowed the beautiful ones. Pharaoh awoke but soon fell asleep again. This time he saw in his dream seven ears of corn full and rank, growing on one stalk; then seven thin, windbeaten ears sprang up on another stalk, and devoured the first ones. These strange dreams worried Pharaoh, and he called all the famous magicians, astrologers, and sages of his country and asked them for the correct interpretation of his dreams. But try as they would, they could not satisfy Pharaoh. They only got the king more worried and nervous by their contradictory and fantastic explanations.

Finally, the Chief Butler remembered Joseph and how he had proved himself a true interpreter of dreams. The Chief Butler, therefore, told his master about the dreams he and the Chief Baker had had in prison, and how a young Hebrew slave had interpreted them correctly. Pharaoh immediately sent for Joseph.

JOSEPH INTERPRETS PHARAOH'S DREAMS: Joseph was thirty years old when he appeared before King Pharaoh. When Pharaoh told him that he had heard of Joseph's great gift as an interpreter of dreams, Joseph modestly replied that his wisdom was not of his own making but of G-d's. Then Pharaoh related his dreams to Joseph, and Joseph knew at once that G-d had revealed their meaning to him.

Joseph informed Pharoah that both dreams had the same meaning, and that G-d wished to tell Pharaoh what He was about to do. Seven years of plenty and abundance would come to Egypt, but they would be followed by seven years of famine. Hunger and privation would be so great that the abundance of the preceding years would be completely swallowed up and forgotten. The fact that Pharaoh had seen the same thing twice meant that G-d had definitely decided to have his dream come true within the very near future. It was now the task of King Pharaoh, Joseph continued, to find a wise and honest man to administrate and control the economy of the land during the seven years of abundance, so that sufficient provisions would be stored away for the seven lean years to come, thereby averting a terrible catastrophe.

JOSEPH RECEIVES GREAT HONORS: This explanation and advice profoundly impressed Pharaoh and his council. Pharaoh decided that he could not find a better and wiser man than Joseph himself, who was blessed by G-d with prophetic wisdom. He immediately appointed Joseph Viceroy of Egypt, second only to the king. Joseph was dressed in royal raiment, and the king gave him the royal signet ring and a golden chain as tokens of his position. In the royal chariot, Joseph, now given an Egyptian name, Tzophenath Paneach, was led through the land, accompanied by a royal suite and heralds, who hailed the new Viceroy and proclaimed his authority. The entire country paid homage to Tzophenath Paneach, and he soon became very popular among the people of Egypt.

JOSEPH IN OFFICE: In accordance with his own advice, Joseph instituted a strict control over the entire food production of Egypt. The seven years of abundance began immediately, and Joseph had large storehouses erected all over the country. Then he bought up most of the surplus that had flooded the markets and stored it away in warehouses. The people too, followed his example and stocked up, for they believed in the truth of Joseph's prediction. But since the people did not take all the necessary precautions to preserve the food over the long period, their stores were spoiled by the time the lean years arrived.

The seven years of plenty passed and the years of famine began; now the entire country found itself dependent upon the provisions stored away by the state, under the wise administration of Joseph. In exchange for food, the people sold their livestock and land, and by the end of the famine, Pharaoh was in complete control of the entire country, and all the people were his serfs, working for him and depending on him for their needs.

23. JOSEPH'S BROTHERS COME TO EGYPT

JOSEPH PREPARES FOR HIS BROTHERS' ARRIVAL: Not only was Egypt hit by the famine, but also all the neighboring countries, Canaan among them. Many people from near and far came to Egypt to buy provisions, since only in the land of Egypt had the famine been anticipated and prepared for. Naturally Joseph expected to see his brothers any day, coming to purchase food for Jacob's household. In order to make sure that he would not miss them, he ordered all purchasers of food to register as soon as they entered Egypt.

THE HARSH RECEPTION: Thus Joseph knew immediately when his ten older brothers arrived in Egypt to buy corn for their father's house. Only Benjamin did not come. Joseph had his brothers brought before him. Joseph recognized his brothers, but they did not recognize him, for when they had last seen him he was but a youngster, and it would have been difficult for them to imagine that this powerful royal personage was their own brother. Joseph thought of his dreams and of their jealous attitude towards him and decided to test them. Through an interpreter, so that they might not guess his identity, Joseph addressed them harshly.

"Whence do you come?" he asked; and they replied: "We come from Canaan and are here to buy food."

"You are spies!" Joseph accused them.

"No, sir," they replied; "your servants have but come to purchase food. We are twelve brothers and our father is in Canaan; the youngest is at home with our father, and one brother disappeared many years ago."

Joseph pretended that he was not convinced, and told his brothers that he would not let them go away till one of them went to fetch their youngest brother, to prove the truth of their words. Then he had them put into prison.

THE CHANGED BROTHERS: On the third day of their imprisonment, Joseph spoke to his brothers again. He told them that he would not keep them in prison any longer, and that in order that they might have an opportunity to prove their honesty, one of the brothers should remain in prison as a hostage. The rest, however, were instructed to return to Canaan with their food and to bring back their youngest brother.

Joseph could not help overhearing his brothers' conversation, full of distress and regret. They believed that the trouble that had befallen them was a punishment from G-d for their heartlessness on that fateful day when they had thrown Joseph into the pit.

Joseph was overcome with love and pity for his brothers when he saw how sorry they were for their cruelty to him; he withdrew quietly and wept. Then he steeled himself, bathed his eyes, and returned to his brothers with a look upon his face so harsh that it made them wince. He ordered his men to bind Simeon, who was next to the eldest. But Simeon terrified the men, and they were powerless to carry out Joseph's order. Thereupon, Manasseh, Joseph's oldest son, seized Simeon, and bound him. The brothers were taken back by the unusual strength of the young Egyptian prince. Such strength they thought possible only in a descendant of Jacob.

Having secretly ordered that the money his brothers had paid for the food be returned to their sacks, Joseph sent them away, warning them to bring their youngest brother with them the next time they came to Egypt.

THE BROTHERS RETURN HOME: The brothers thanked Joseph and left for Canaan, their mules packed with corn. On the way, they stopped at an inn. One of them opened his sack to take out some fodder for his animal, and was astonished to find that his money had been returned to him. Now they were even more frightened than before, because they felt that more trouble was in store for them.

Arriving home, they told their father everything that had happened. When they emptied the corn, they discovered all the rest of the money they had paid for it, in their sacks. Fear overcame everyone of them. When they told their father that they would have to take Benjamin with them to Egypt in order to save Simeon, he said in great distress, "Joseph is gone, and Simeon is not here; now you want to take Benjamin away. If any mischief should befall him on the way, you will bring my gray head with sorrow to the grave. My son shall not go with you!"

24. THE BROTHERS RETURN TO EGYPT

JUDAH VOUCHES FOR BENJAMIN: The provisions were used up and famine again threatened Jacob's household. Jacob asked his sons to return to Egypt to buy food. "If you do not permit us to take Benjamin along, we cannot go to Egypt," Judah said, "for the man told us not to look upon his face again, unless Benjamin were with us!"

Jacob did not conceal his great anxiety for Benjamin's safety, and finally Judah vouched with his own life for the safety of the boy. With starvation threatening the entire household, Jacob could no longer delay his sons' going to Egypt and permitted Benjamin to go with them. He told his sons to return the money they had found in their sacks, and advised them to take some fine presents for the ruler of Egypt. Then, he blessed them and sent them on their way.

A FRIENDLIER RECEPTION: When the brothers appeared before Joseph, and Joseph saw that Benjamin was among them, he told his steward to bring them into the house, and to prepare a meal for them. The man did so. Joseph's brothers were suspicious of the unexpected hospitality. They approached the supervisor and told him of the strange return of their money when they had first purchased food in Egypt. They assured him that they had brought the money back with them, together with more money for the new purchases. The supervisor allayed their fears, telling them that he had received the money, and that the money they had found in their sacks was a gift from G-d. Then he brought Simeon to them. Simeon told them how well he had been treated, and greatly relieved, they all sat down at the table.

When Joseph arrived, his brothers presented him with the gifts Jacob had sent him. He greeted them cordially and inquired after their aged father. Then he welcomed Benjamin; but on seeing his youngest brother, Joseph was overcome with emotion, and had to withdraw, so that his brothers might not see the tears that were about to burst forth from his eyes.

Returning to his brothers, Joseph presided over the feast. For the first time since they had sold Joseph, the brothers felt really merry and happy, for although they did not know it, there they were, all twelve of them together. Only Joseph knew, and he thought how well it was for brothers to live together in peace and harmony!

Many a time Joseph surprised them by his intimate knowledge of their personal lives. For instance, he seated them according to their age, and called them by their names. He pretended to get all this knowledge from his "divining cup" which he kept putting up to his ear, as if it were revealing many secrets to him. After the meal, Joseph gave them all presents; to Benjamin, however, he gave five times as much as to the others.

25. JOSEPH REVEALS HIS IDENTITY

JOSEPH TESTS HIS BROTHERS: Joseph still wanted to see how much they were willing to sacrifice for one another. After the meal, he told his supervisor to fill the sacks of his brothers with provisions, and again to put their money on top. His own "magic" cup, however, he ordered to be put in Benjamin's sack. The man carried out Joseph's orders, and the next morning, unaware of the plot, Joseph's brothers set out for Canaan, happy that everything had gone so well.

Hardly had they left the city, when the supervisor came riding after them and reprimanded them for stealing his master's "divining cup." What ingratitude for the kindness with which he had treated them! In vain did they protest, reminding him that they had even returned the money they had found in their sacks the last time. Why should they now steal what belonged to his master? They agreed to have their belongings searched, and said that if one of them had stolen the cup, he would die, and that the others would serve as slaves.

The supervisor, however, said that the thief alone would be held responsible and taken into bondage, and that the rest could go home free.

Convinced of their innocence, the brothers unloaded their packs. The search began with the oldest and went down to the youngest. When Benjamin's sack was opened, the brothers were aghast. There the cup lay, mute evidence of a crime they knew Benjamin could not have committed. Tearing their clothes in great despair, the brothers decided they would stick together, one for all and all for one. How different they were now from what they had been many years earlier, when they had turned deaf ears to Joseph's plight!

All the brothers now returned to Egypt to try to save the innocent Benjamin.

JUDAH PLEADS FOR BENJAMIN: When the brothers returned to Joseph, they fell down before him and proclaimed their innocence. They could not understand how such a thing had happened, they said, and expressed the belief that the discovery of the cup in Benjamin's sack was some kind of punishment for their sins; they added that they were ready to take the consequence—they would all be Joseph's slaves!

But Joseph refused their offer and said that only the one in whose possession the cup had been found was to remain as slave; the others could return to their father in Canaan.

Then Judah stepped forward and began to plead for Benjamin. Judah began by accusing the harsh Viceroy of a plot to enslave them from the start. He warned him of the unusual strength of the sons of Jacob. Cleverly, Joseph replied that his divining cup had already told him that two of them had destroyed a whole city, but that he was not impressed.

Then Judah changed his tactics and appealed to Joseph's heart. He recounted the whole story of Jacob and his two beloved sons, whom his favorite wife, Rachel, had borne him in his old age. Judah told of his father's grief when one of them had disappeared from home. He revealed that should they come home without the other one, their aged father would never survive the calamity. Finally, Judah offered himself in the boy's place, pointing out that he would be of so much more value than Benjamin as a slave.

JOSEPH REVEALS HIMSELF: Judah's moving appeal and spirit of self-sacrifice in behalf of his brother well nigh tore Joseph's tender heart asunder. He knew that his brothers had changed completely, and that they would rather die than give Benjamin away as a slave. Joseph could now forgive them for all they had done to him, which, after all, he knew was for the best. Joseph felt that he could no longer play the hateful role he had assumed in order to test his brothers. His tears were bursting forth, and he longed to embrace his beloved brothers. Sending all the Egyptian courtiers and attendants out of the room, Joseph, with tears in his eyes, exclaimed in Hebrew, in a voice shaking with emotion: "I am Joseph! Is my father still alive?"

So stunned were his brothers that they could not answer him. Joseph realized their embarrassment and possible fear of him, and he continued to talk to them with brotherly affection which soon put them at ease. He told them not to worry about having sold him as a slave, for it had been G-d's will to send him to Egypt to save their lives from hunger. Then he asked them to hurry back to Jacob and tell him that they had found his lost son, Joseph. He asked them to tell their father that despite the many years of absence from home, in an environment of idolatry and immorality, he had remained the same Joseph his father had known and loved. Joseph thereupon begged his father to come to Egypt with his whole household, where Joseph would take care of them. In Goshen, a province of Egypt, they could settle and live in peace and plenty, for the years of famine were not yet over. There he would take care of them as best he could.

Joseph embraced his brother Benjamin and kissed him, and then he embraced all his other brothers. All eyes were full of tears, tears of happiness and of gratitude to G-d for His boundless mercy.

26. JACOB AND HIS FAMILY GO TO EGYPT

RETURN OF THE BROTHERS: The news of Joseph's discovery of his brothers was welcomed by King Pharaoh. He urged Joseph to bring the entire family to Egypt and to give them the best of the land.

Laden with presents, and accompanied by a whole

caravan of wagons for the removal of the family, the brothers hastened home to bring the happy tidings to their father.

Jacob's heart stood still as he heard the wonderful news. He could hardly believe that his beloved Joseph was still alive. However, when Jacob saw the gifts his sons brought with them, and especially when he heard the special message Joseph had sent him, reminding his father of their last scholarly discussion before Joseph departed in search of his brothers on that fateful day, Jacob knew that Joseph was alive. Jacob felt like a changed man. He was greatly cheered and strengthened by the good tidings, and immediateiy prepared for the journey to Egypt, for he wanted to see Joseph before he died.

ON THE WAY TO EGYPT: With his entire household of seventy persons, Jacob left his native land, but not before he had visited Beer-Sheba, where he offered sacrifices to G-d. Here G-d appeared to him and told him not to be afraid to go to Egypt, because He would be with him and eventually turn his small family into a great nation; then He would bring them back from Egypt and they would settle in the land of Canaan.

From Beer-Sheba Jacob continued his journey to Egypt. He sent Judah before him to make preparations for the arrival of the family, and especially to set up a school and an academy for the children.

JACOB MEETS JOSEPH: When Joseph heard that his father w.u coming, he prepared a big reception. All of Egypt was celebrating the arrival of their Viceroy's father. Joseph himself went to meet his father on the way. When Joseph saw his father from a distance, he stepped down from his royal chariot and ran forward to greet him. They embraced each other affectionately and shed many tears over their long separation. Finally, Jacob said: "Now that I have seen your face again, I can die in peace."

JACOB VISITS PHARAOH: Soon after his father's arrival, Joseph went to Pharaoh and told him that his father and brothers had arrived with all their possessions. Pharaoh was very pleased and granted them the land of Goshen for residence. Then Joseph introduced his father and brothers to the king. Pharaoh, impressed with Jacob's wisdom and patriarchal appearance, asked him how old he was. Jacob replied that he was one hundred and thirty years old; that most of these years had been full of sorrow and pain, but that now he was looking forward to his happiest years. Jacob then blessed Pharaoh.

Joseph gave his father and brothers good land in Goshen, where they settled to live in peace and were provided with everything they needed. When the years of famine were over, the land gradually returned to normal. However, every one knew that if it had not been for Joseph, the entire population would have perished of starvation.

Joseph married Osnath, Dinah's daughter, who had been brought up in the house of Potiphar. She bore him two children, Manasseh and Ephraim. When his father settled in Goshen, Joseph sent his two sons to stay with their grandfather to be insructed in the knowledge of G-d.

JACOB'S LAST REQUEST: Jacob lived in Goshen for seventeen years. When he felt that his end was approaching, he sent for Joseph and had him swear not to bury him in Egypt, but to take him back to Canaan and lay him to rest with his fathers, in the Cave of Machpelah.

JACOB BLESSES JOSEPH'S CHILDREN: One day Joseph was told that his father was seriously ill. Joseph took his two sons, Manasseh and Ephraim, and went to see Jacob.

The aged Jacob was lying on his sick-bed. It was the first case of sickness before death, for hitherto people had died suddenly of old age. Jacob, however, had prayed to G-d that death come not unexpectedly, in order that man might have a chance to look back upon his life and make amends through timely repentance.

When Joseph entered his room, Jacob raised himself in his bed and greeted him. Then he blessed Joseph and put Ephraim and Manasseh on an equal footing with his own sons, giving them rights equal to those of Reuben and Simeon. Thus he made Ephraim and Manasseh members of the twelve tribes. (They took the place of Joseph and Levi). Then he placed his hands on the heads of his two grandchildren, and said: "The angel who has redeemed me from all evil will bless the children, and let in them my name be called and the names of my fathers Abraham and Isaac and may they multiply in the midst of the earth. With you shall everyone in Israel bless his children, saying, 'G-d make thee as Ephraim and Manasseh.' "

JACOB'S DEATH: Then Jacob called all his sons together to bless them.

Admonishing his children to keep together and to remain staunch in their belief in G-d, Jacob died, after he had again told them to bury him in the Cave of Machpelah. Jacob was one hundred and forty-seven years old when G-d took his holy soul back to heaven.

JACOB'S BURIAL: All of Egypt mourned with Joseph over the passing of Jacob, who, in the time of his stay in Goshen, had gained the esteem and love of all the people. Jacob's children fulfilled their promise and carried the coffin all the way to Canaan. When the procession reached the border of Canaan, thirty-one kings turned out to pay homage to the dead. Esau, too, heard of his brother's death, and came to accompany his body to its place of rest. Finally they reached Hebron and made preparations to bury Jacob in the Cave of Machpelah.

ESAU'S DEATH: Esau did not want to give permission to bury Jacob in the Cave of Machpelah. He wanted to reserve the place next to his father Isaac and his grandfather Abraham for himself, even though twenty-seven years before, when he and Jacob had divided the inheritance of their father, he had sold Jacob all rights to the land. Fighting broke out between Esau's men and the sons of Jacob in which forty of Esau's people were killed. Hushim, the son of Dan, who was hard of hearing, had been sitting by the hearse of his dead grandfather. When he finally heard the noise of fighting and observed the delay of the burial, he asked for the reason. He did not understand exactly what had happened. He heard only that Esau withheld permission for Jacob's burial. He took a sword, ran into the camp, and slew Esau. Esau's head fell to the floor and was buried in the Cave of Machpelah, where his ancestors had found their last rest. His body was taken back to his home in Seir.

JOSEPH'S PLEDGE TO HIS BROTHERS: After Jacob's death, his sons became afraid that Joseph might now take revenge for the evil they had committed against him in his youth. So they sent word to him, telling him that before his death their father had asked them to tell him that he should forgive his brothers for what they had done to him. Joseph, however, calmed their fears and told them not to worry about the past, adding that it had been G-d's will that had turned everything just the right way. He assured them of his undying love and loyalty, and pledged to sustain them and their families. They were all greatly moved by his words, and their eyes were filled with tears.

JOSEPH'S DEATH: When Joseph felt that his end was coming, he asked his brothers to swear that when G-d took them out of Egypt and brought them back to Canaan, the land that G-d had promised to Abraham, Isaac, and Jacob, they would take his bones along. This the brothers promised on oath, which was to be upheld by their children from generation to generation, until the day of their departure from Egypt.

Joseph died at the age of one hundred and ten years. He was embalmed and put into a sarcophage that was let down into the Nile river. (The Egyptians hoped that the children of Israel would never be able to fulfill their promise, and would thus have to remain in Egypt. But before the Jews left Egypt, Moses went looking for Joseph's casket. Serach, the daughter of Asher, who was a prophetess, showed him the place where the sarcophage had been immersed in the water. Moses called to Joseph, and the casket rose from the water. During all the years of wandering through the desert, the children of Israel carried Joseph's bones along, until they brought them to the promised land, where they were laid to rest).

END OF BOOK ONE

TEST YOUR KNOWLEDGE

1. Why did the brothers not get on very well with Joseph? (p. 61)

2. Did Joseph interpret his own dreams? (p. 61)

3. How did Joseph get to Egypt? (p. 63)

4. Whose were the first dreams Joseph interpreted? (p. 64)

5. Who was Tzophenath Paneach? (p. 67)

6. Had the brothers changed, in appearance and character, when Joseph saw them in Egypt? (p. 69)

7. Who said, "You will bring my gray head with sorrow to the grave," and why? (p. 70)

8. When did all twelve sons of Jacob first sit down together to enjoy a feast in peace and harmony? (p. 72)

9. What made Joseph finally reveal his identity to his brothers? (p. 74)

10. What proof of Joseph's existence did the brothers bring to their father? (p. 76)

11. Where did the children of Israel settle in Egypt? (p. 77)

12. Whom did Joseph marry? (p. 77)

13. What is the traditional blessing bestowed upon Jewish children, and who were the first to get it? (p. 78)

14. What did Jacob admonish his children before his death? (p. 79)

15. How old was Esau when he died? (p. 79)

16. What pledge did Joseph exact from his brothers before his death? (p. 80)

17. Where was Joseph buried?

BOOK TWO

IV. ISRAEL IN EGYPTIAN BONDAGE

27. ISRAEL'S ENSLAVEMENT

BEGINNING OF OPPRESSION: Joseph and his brothers died, and the children of Israel multiplied in the land of Egypt. They held important positions and played an important rôle in the political, cultural, and economic life of the country. It is not surprising that they stirred the jealousy of the native Egyptians who felt outshone by the "foreigners."

Old King Pharaoh died, too, and a new king ascended the throne. He had no sympathy or love for the children of Israel, and chose to forget all that Joseph had done for Egypt. He decided to take action against the growing influence and numbers of the children of Israel. He called his council together, and they advised him to enslave these people and oppress them before they grew too powerful. Pharaoh limited the personal freedom of the Hebrews, put heavy taxes on them, and recruited their men into forced labor battalions under the supervision of harsh taskmasters. Thus the children of Israel had to build cities, erect monuments, construct roads, work in the quarries, and hew stones or make bricks and tiles. But the more the Egyptians oppressed them, and the harder the restrictions imposed upon them became, the more the children of Israel increased and multiplied. Finally, when King Pharaoh saw that forcing the Hebrews to do hard work did not succeed in suppressing their rapidly growing numbers, he decreed that all newly born male children of the Hebrews be thrown into the Nile River. Only daughters should be permitted to live.

Thus Pharaoh hoped to end the numerical increase of the Jewish population, and at the same time to eliminate a danger which, according to the predictions of his astrologers, threatened his own life in the person of a leader to be born to the children of Israel.

THE LEVITES: The only group of Jews that escaped enslavement was the tribe of Levi. Levi was the last of Jacob's sons to die, and his influence over his tribe was great and lasting. They had taken over the Torah academy Jacob had established in Goshen, and they instructed the children of Israel in the knowledge of G-d and His holy teachings. Thus they were occupied with spiritual matters and did not mix with the Egyptians, while many of their brethren had given up their old customs and way of life. Except for their language, clothing, and names, many of the children of Israel had become assimilated into the social and cultural environment of their Egyptian neighbors, and they were the ones to arouse the wrath of the Egyptians. Only the children of Levi were, therefore, spared the slavery and oppression which the Egyptians imposed upon the rest of Israel.

28. THE BIRTH OF MOSES

MOSES' PARENTS: Levi's grandson, Amram, the son of Kehot, married Jochebed, and she bore him three children. Their first child was a girl by the name of Miriam, who was later to become a great prophetess of the Jewish people. The second child was Aaron, the highest priest of G-d, famous for his extraordinary love of peace. Next to his brother Moses, he was the greatest leader of our nation in his time. It was Amram's youngest son Moses who was destined to lead the children of Israel from Egypt and to receive for them the Holy Torah on Mount Sinai.

THE BIRTH OF MOSES: The day approached when, according to the Egyptian astrologers, the liberator of the children of Israel was to be born. Since they did not know whether he would be of Jewish or Egyptian descent, all male children born that day, were to be thrown into the water by order of King Pharaoh. This same day, the seventh of Adar, Jochebed, Amram's wife, gave birth to her third child, a boy. Right from the first moment of his birth, it became apparent that he was an extraordinary child, for the house was filled with a radiant light. His parents tried everything possible to prevent his falling into the hands of Pharaoh's men, who were continuously searching for newborn Jewish children. After three months, Jochebed saw that she would not be able to conceal her child any longer. She therefore made a small, water-proof basket in which she put the child and set him down among the papyrus reeds growing on the brink of the Nile. While Jochebed tearfully returned home, her daughter Miriam remained nearby to watch the baby.

MOSES SAVED: The day was hot, and King Pharaoh's daughter, Bithya, came out to the river, accompanied by her maids, to take a bath in the cool waters of the Nile. Suddenly she heard the wailing of a small child. Presently she found the basket, and in it an infant boy. Intrigued by the child's beauty, Bithya tried to figure out a way to enable her to keep him for herself and save him from death, for she understood that this boy was one of the children born to a Jewish family, and therefore condemned to death.

The child refused to be nursed by any of the Egyptian maids-in-waiting, and continued to weep. At this moment, Miriam came over to the princess and offered to procure for the child a Jewish nurse, who would keep it as long as the princess thought necessary. Bithya was glad of this solution. Miriam rushed home and brought her mother, whom she introduced as an experienced nurse.

For two years the baby was left in his mother's care. Meanwhile Bithya told Pharaoh about the boy she had found and adopted. Her father did not object, although the foundling was of Jewish descent; for his astrologers had told him that the one who, according to the constellation of the stars, had been predestined to become the liberator of the Jews and to threaten the life of King Pharaoh, had already been placed at the mercy of the water. Moreover, they further said, it was the fate of this boy to die because of water.* Thus, they felt sure that the danger had already been averted. Moses was taken to the royal court, where he grew up as the princely adopted son of King Pharaoh's daughter.

MOSES BECOMES TONGUE-TIED: Once it happened that Moses was playing on King Pharaoh's lap. He saw the shining crown, studded with jewels, and reached for it and took it off. Pharaoh, who was superstitious like all his fellow-Egyptians, and who in addition was always afraid of losing his throne, asked his astrologers and counsellors for the meaning of this action of the infant. Most of them interpreted it to mean that Moses was a threat to Pharaoh's crown and suggested that the child be put to death before it could do any

---

* See ch. 45

A VIEW OF THE NILE

harm. One of the king's counsellors, however, suggested that they should first test the boy and see whether his action was prompted by intelligence, or he was merely grasping for sparkling things as any other child would.

Pharaoh agreed to this, and two bowls were set down before young Moses. One contained gold and jewels, and the other held glowing firecoals. Moses reached out for the gold, but an angel directed his hand to the coals. Moses snatched a glowing coal and put it to his lips. He burned his hand and tongue, but his life was saved. After that fateful test, Moses suffered from a slight speech defect. He could not become an orator, but his words were to carry weight withal, for it was G-d's words that were spoken through his lips.

29. MOSES' EARLY ADVENTURES

MOSES FLEES EGYPT: Moses grew older and began to take a personal interest in the suffering of his brethren, the children of Israel. He made it his business to go out to Goshen, to talk with the slaving Jews and try to alleviate their plight as much as possible. Often he put his hands and shoulders to work to ease the burden of an aged Hebrew. Through his influence with Pharaoh, who appreciated and esteemed Moses' wisdom, effective measures to ease the plight of the slaves were introduced little by little, for Moses had to be careful not to arouse Pharaoh's suspicions. One of these measures was to grant the slaves a day of rest, and Moses saw to it that this day was Shabbos.

One day Moses went again to Goshen to bring hope and courage to his fellow Jews, amongst whom he had become very popular. They appreciated his friendliness and

the help he could give them, and they were astonished at
his keen mind and the readiness with which he learned
and mastered the knowledge of the holy teachings of
the Levites. That day he happened to observe a scene
not uncommon in Goshen. An Egyptian overseer in
charge of ten Jewish labor squads, each under a Jewish
supervisor, hit one of his charges. Seeing that the Egyptian
was persecuting the Hebrew unjustly, Moses came to his
rescue and killed the persecutor. Having assured himself
that there was nobody who had witnessed this scene, he
buried the body in the sand and returned to Pharaoh's
palace.

Soon, therafter, he visited Goshen again. This time he
saw two Hebrews quarelling. When he warned one of them
not to raise his hand against a fellow-Jew, he retorted:
"Who made you chief and judge over us? Perhaps you
intend to kill me, as you killed the Egyptian?" It grieved
Moses to see that there was such a wicked and irresponsible
person among his fellow Jews, and he knew, moreover,
that his life was now in danger. Indeed, one of these men
betrayed Moses to Pharaoh, and Moses was condemned to
death for the slaying of the Egyptian taskmaster. But as
the executioner's axe came down on Moses' neck, a wonderful miracle happened. Moses' neck became as hard as
rock, and the axe bounced back. In the confusion that
followed, Moses escaped and fled to the land of Cush.
There he stayed for many years, and because of his intelligence and wisdom, became the king of the natives.

**MOSES IN
MIDIAN:**   A conspiracy and upheaval in the government of Cush forced Moses to flee again, and
he went to Midian. The priest of Midian,
Jethro, had once been one of King Pharaoh's foremost ad-
viser's, but because of his friendly attitude towards the

Hebrews, he had to leave Pharaoh's court. Jethro then settled in Midian, and became the highest priest of the land. A man of great intelligence, Jethro soon realized the silliness of idol-worship, and gave up his priesthood. The people of Midian began to hate their erstwhile priest and persecuted him. Often it happened that Jethro's daughters were driven away from the communal well when they came to water the flocks of their father, and had to wait to the very last, until the other shepherds were gone.

On the day Moses arrived in Midian, he saw the rough shepherds chase the daughters of Jethro away from the well. Moses stood up for the girls, and helped them water their sheep. On that day they returned to Jethro rather early, and he was astonished to see them back so soon. His daughters told him about the unexpected help. Jethro immediately invited Moses to his house and not long thereafter he gave him his oldest daughter Zipporah for a wife. Zipporah bore Moses two children. The first one he called Gershom ("a stranger there") in commemoration of the fact that he was a stranger and exile in the land of Midian, and the second he called Eliezer, "G-d is my helper," in gratitude for G-d's protection.

30. THE DIVINE AMBASSADOR

G-D UPHOLDS THE COVENANT: The children of Israel could no longer endure their terrible suffering and persecution at the hands of their cruel overlords. Their cries for help, their supplications and prayers, coming from the very bottom of their hearts, pierced the heavens. G-d remembered His convenant with Abraham, Isaac, and Jacob, and decided to deliver their descendants from bondage.

G-D REVEALS HIMSELF TO MOSES: Moses took care of the flocks of his father-in-law Jethro. Once when he had driven his flocks far out in the desert, a small lamb got lost. After searching for it all over the hills of the desert, Moses found it near the Mount of Horeb. He took the tired little animal in his arms and set out to return to the flocks. Suddenly an unusual sight attracted his attenion.

He saw a thornbush burst out in flame, but although the flames burned continuously, the bush did not turn into ashes. His curiosity aroused, Moses stepped closer, and out of the thornbush, he heard the voice of G-d calling: "Moses, Moses!"

"Here I am," replied Moses.

G-d continued to speak to him saying: "Do not draw closer! Take off your shoes from your feet; for the place whereon you stand is holy ground. I am the G-d of your father, of Abraham, Isaac, and Jacob." Moses covered his face; for he was afraid to look up to G-d.

G-d then told Moses that He had heard the lamentations of the children of Israel in distress; and that He would deliver them from the hands of the Egyptian oppressors and bring them back into the Promised Land, a land flowing with milk and honey. He, Moses, was the one to go to Pharaoh and lead the Jewish people out of Egypt.

Moses hesitated to accept this great mission. He was afraid he was neither worthy nor able to carry out such a great task. G-d assured him, however, that He would be with him. Still Moses begged to be relieved of this mission. He feared that the children of Israel would not recognize his authority to speak as their leader. If he told them that G-d had sent him, they would demand to know His name.

Thereupon G-d told Moses to identify Him to the children of Israel as the G-d of their fathers Abraham, Isaac, and Jacob, Who has now come to redeem them from slavery and take them to the land He had promised their ancestors.

THE MIRACULOUS SIGNS: To further impress the children of Israel, Moses was to perform for them miraculous wonders with his staff. It was the staff that Adam had taken out of the Garden of Eden, and that had served Noah, Abraham, Isaac, and Jacob. It had the inscription of G-d's Holy Name on it. Jethro had taken possession of this wonderful staff after Joseph's death. He planted it in his garden and no one had since that time been able to pull it out of the earth, until Moses came and removed it easily, thus proving his just claim to its ownership.

Now G-d told Moses to throw this staff on the ground. Moses did so, and the staff turned into a serpent. Moses fled in terror, but G-d ordered him to grasp it by its tail: Moses did so, and the serpent changed back into a staff.

Again G-d bade Moses put his hand into his bosom. When Moses took it out it was stricken with incurable leprosy. Then he again put his hand into his bosom, and when he pulled it out, it was clean as before. Finally, G-d told Moses that if he were to pour water on dry land it would turn into blood. All these signs G-d gave to Moses to be able to impress upon the children of Israel that G-d had sent him to them.

Moses made a final attempt to be relieved of his mission, hoping that G-d Himself would bring about His people's salvation. "I am tongue-tied," Moses pleaded. But G-d told him that the One who gave the human being

the ability to hear, see, and speak, could surely remedy this
handicap! He then told Moses that Aaron would serve
as his spokesman. Then G-d ordered Moses to return
to Egypt, since there was no longer any danger for him
there.

31. MOSES RETURNS TO EGYPT

**MOSES ACCEPTED
AS LEADER:**
Moses returned to his father-in-
law in Midian, and asked for his
approval to return to his brethren
in Egypt. Jethro gave him his blessing, and Moses set out
for Egypt. G-d then ordered Aaron to meet Moses. They
met in the desert by Mount Horeb, where Moses told his
older brother of the great Divine mission they were to
carry out.

Back in Goshen, they visited the sages and leaders of
the children of Israel. Having performed the miracles as
G-d had instructed Moses, they told the people of the good
tidings. The children of Israel believed in the Divine mission of the sons of Amram, and new hopes and faith filled
their hearts.

**MOSES AND AARON
BEFORE PHARAOH:**
Moses was eighty years old, and
his brother eighty-three, when
they entered the palace of King
Pharaoh. Fearlessly, they went past the heavy guard of
men and wild animals that surrounded his inner chambers,
and which permitted no unbidden visitor to enter. Nobody had ever been able to see the King of Egypt in person,
and speak to him, except his astrologers and counsellors.
Astonished and frightened by their sudden appearance,
Pharaoh asked the two brothers what they wanted. The
message sounded like a command: "Thus has the Lord G-d
of Israel said, 'Let My people go, that they may feast to
Me in the desert.' " Pharaoh haughtily refused, saying that

he had never heard of the G-d of the Israelites, and that His name was not registered in his lists of gods of all nations. He further accused Moses and Aaron of a conspiracy against the government, and of interference with the work of the Hebrew slaves. The miracles they performed in his presence did not greatly impress him, for his magicians could do almost as well.

On the same day Pharaoh ordered his supervisors to increase the demands on the children of Israel and to make their burden still heavier. If they had time to think of liberty and worship of G-d and similar ideas, quite unbecoming of slaves, then they must be getting too much leisure, Pharaoh thought. Whereas they had been supplied with the raw materials heretofore, they now had not only to produce the same amount of labor, but in addition, they had to procure their own raw materials for the bricks. The children of Israel were physically unable to cope with such an impossible task, and they suffered even more than before. In desperation the children of Israel bitterly reproached Moses and Aaron for making their fate even worse, instead of helping them.

Deeply hurt and disappointed, Moses prayed to G-d. G-d consoled him and assured him that his mission eventually would be successful, but not before Pharaoh and all of Egypt would be smitten by terrible plagues, in order to be adequately punished for oppressing the children of Israel. The children of Israel would then also see and recognize their true and faithful G-d.

32. THE TEN PLAGUES

1—BLOOD: When Pharaoh persisted in his refusal to liberate the children of Israel, Moses and Aaron warned him that G-d would punish both him and his people. First, the waters of the land of Egypt were to be turned into blood. Moses walked with Aaron to the brink of the river. There Aaron raised his staff, smote the water, and converted them into streams of blood. All the people of Egypt and the King himself beheld this miracle; they saw the fish die as the blood flowed over the land, and they turned with disgust from the offensive smell of the sacred river. It was impossible for them to drink of the water of the Nile, far-famed for its delicious taste; and they tried to dig deep into the ground for water. Unfortunately for the Egyptians, not only the floods of the Nile but all the waters of Egypt, wherever they were, turned to blood. The fish died in the rivers and lakes, and for a whole week man and beast suffered horrible thirst. Yet Pharaoh would not give in.

2—FROGS: After due warning, the second plague came to Egypt. Aaron stretched forth his hand over the waters of Egypt, and frogs swarmed forth. They covered every inch of land and entered the houses and bedrooms; wherever an Egyptian turned, whatever he touched, he found there the slimy bodies of frogs, the croakings of which filled the air. Now Pharaoh became frightened, and he asked Moses and Aaron to pray to G-d to remove the nuisance, promising that he would liberate the Jewish people at once. But as soon as the frogs disappeared, he broke his promise and refused to let the children of Israel go.

3—BUGS: Then G-d ordered Aaron to smite the dust of the earth with his staff, and no sooner did he do so than all over Egypt bugs crawled forth from the dust to cover the land. Man and beast suffered untold misery from this terrible plague. Although his counsellors pointed out that this surely was G-d's punishment, Pharaoh steeled his heart and remained relentless in his determination to keep the children of Israel in bondage.

4—WILD ANIMALS: The fourth plague to harass the Egyptians consisted of hordes of wild animals roving all over the country, and destroying everything in their path. Only the province of Goshen where the children of Israel dwelt was immune from this as well as from the other plagues. Again Pharaoh promised faithfully to let the Hebrews go out into the desert on the condition that they would not go too far. Moses prayed to G-d, and the wild animals disappeared. But as soon as they had gone, Pharaoh withdrew his promise and refused Moses' demand.

5—PESTILENCE: Then G-d sent a fatal pestilence that killed most of the domestic animals of the Egyptians. How the people must have grieved when they saw their stately horses, the pride of Egypt, perish; when all the cattle of the fields were stricken at the word of Moses; and when the animals upon which they looked as gods died smitten by the plague! They had, moreover, the mortification of seeing the beasts of the Israelites unhurt. Yet Pharaoh still hardened his heart, and would not let the Israelites go.

6—BOILS: Then followed the sixth plague, which was so painful and loathsome that it must have struck the people of Egypt with horror and agony. G-d commanded Moses to take soot from the furnaces, and to sprinkle it towards heaven; and as Moses did so, boils burst forth upon man and beast throughout the land of Egypt.

7—HAIL: Now, Moses announced to the king that a hail-storm of unprecedented violence was to sweep the land; no living thing, no tree, no herb was to escape its fury unhurt; safety was to be found only in the shelter of the houses; those, therefore, who believed and were afraid might keep in their homes, and drive their cattle into the sheds. Some of the Egyptians took this counsel to heart; but the reckless and the stubborn left their cattle with their servants in the fields. When Moses stretched forth his staff, the hail poured down with violence; deafening thunder rolled over the earth, and lightning rent the heavens, and ran like fire along the ground. The hail did its work of destruction; man and beast who were exposed to its rage died on the spot; the herbs were scattered to the wind, and the trees lay shattered on the ground. But the land of Goshen, untouched by the ravages of the storm, bloomed like a garden amidst the general devastation. Then Pharaoh sent for Moses and acknowledged his sins. "The Lord is righteous," he said, "and I and my people are wicked. Entreat the Lord that there should be no more thundering and hail; and I will let you go, and you shall stay no longer."

Moses replied: "When I am gone out of the city, I shall spread out my hands to the Lord; and the thunder will cease, and neither will there be any more hail, that thou mayest know that the earth is the Lord's." And it happened as Moses had said: the storm ceased—but Pharaoh's heart remained hardened.

8—LOCUST: The next time Moses and Aaron came before Pharaoh, he appeared somewhat relenting, and asked them who was to participate in the worship the Israelites wanted to hold in the desert. When they told him that everyone without exception, young and old, men and women, and animals, were to go, Pharaoh suggested that only the men should go, and that the women and children, as well as all their possessions should remain in Egypt. Moses and Aaron would not accept this offer, and Pharaoh became angry and ordered them to leave his palace. Before leaving, Moses warned him of new and untold suffering. But Pharaoh remained adamant, even though his advisers counselled against further resistance.

As soon as Moses left the palace, he raised his arms toward heaven and an east wind brought swarms of locusts into Egypt, covering the sun, and devouring everything green that had escaped the hail and previous plagues. Never in the history of mankind had there been such a devastating plague of locusts as this one. It brought complete ruin upon Egypt, which had already been thoroughly ravaged by the previous catastrophes. Again Pharaoh sent for Moses and Aaron, and implored them to pray to G-d to stop the plague. Moses complied, and G-d sent a strong west wind that drove the locusts into the sea. When relief came, Pharaoh's obstinacy returned to him, and he refused to liberate the people of Israel.

9—DARKNESS: Then followed the ninth plague. For several days all of Egypt was enveloped in a thick and impenetrable veil of darkness which extinguished all lights kindled. The Egyptians were gripped with fear, and remained glued to their places wherever they stood or sat. Only in Goshen, where the children of Israel dwelt, there was light. But not all of the Jews were saved from this plague. There were a few who wanted to be regarded as Egyptians rather than as members of the Hebrew race, and who tried, therefore, to imitate the Egyptians in everything, or, as we call it, to assimilate themselves. They did not want to leave Egypt. These people died during the days of darkness.

Again Pharaoh tried to bargain with Moses and Aaron, bidding them depart with all their people, leaving their flocks and herds behind as a pledge. Moses and Aaron informed him, however, that they would accept nothing less than complete freedom for the men, women, and children, and that they were to take all their belongings with them. Now Pharaoh became angry and ordered Moses and Aaron to leave and never to return. He warned them that if they were to come before him again they would die. Moses replied that it would not be necessary for them to see Pharaoh, for G-d would send one more plague over Egypt, after which Pharaoh would give his unconditional permission for the children of Israel to leave Egypt. Exactly at midnight, Moses continued, G-d would pass over Egypt and smite all first-born, man and beast. Of the children of Israel, however, nobody was to die. A bitter cry would sweep Egypt, and all the Egyptians would be gripped with terror, lest they all die. Then Pharaoh himself would come to seek out the leaders of the Hebrews, and beg them to leave Egypt without delay!

With these words, Moses and Aaron left Pharaoh, who was seething with rage.

THE PASSOVER SACRIFICE: On the first day of the month of Nissan, two weeks before the Exodus from Egypt, G-d said to Moses and Aaron: "This month shall be unto you the beginning of months; it shall be the first month of the year to you. Speak ye unto all the congregation of Israel saying: 'In the tenth day of this month they shall take to them every man a lamb . . . a lamb for a household . . . and ye shall keep it until the fourteenth day of the same month; and the whole assembly of the congregation of Israel shall kill it at dusk. And they shall take of the blood, and put it on the two side-posts and on the lintel, upon the houses wherein they shall eat it. And they shall eat the flesh in that night, roast with fire, and unleavened bread; with bitter herbs they shall eat it. . . . And ye shall let nothing of it remain until the morning; but that which remaineth of it until the morning ye shall burn with fire. And thus shall ye eat it: with your loins girded, your shoes on your feet and your staff in your hand; and ye shall eat in haste—it is Passover dedicated to the Lord. And when I see the blood, I will pass over you, and there shall be no plague upon you to destroy you, when I smite the land of Egypt. And this day shall be unto you for a memorial, and ye shall celebrate it as a feast unto the Lord, throughout your generations. Seven days shall ye eat unleavened bread, and put away all leaven from your houses. And it shall be when your children shall say unto you: What is the meaning of this service? Ye shall say: It is the sacrifice of the Passover unto G-d who passed over the houses of the children of Israel in Egypt when he smote the Egyptians but delivered our houses!"

Moses told all this to the children of Israel. It required a great deal of faith and courage for the children of Israel to carry out this Command, for the lamb was a sacred animal to the ancient Egyptians. But the children of Israel eagerly and fearlessly carried out all that G-d had ordered.

10—DEATH OF THE FIRST-BORN: Midnight of the fourteenth to the fifteenth of Nissan came, and G-d smote all first-born in the land of Egypt, from the first-born of King Pharaoh, down to the first-born of a captive in the dungeon, and all the first-born of the cattle, exactly as Moses had warned. There was a loud and bitter wail—in each house a loved one lay fatally stricken. Then Pharaoh called for Moses and

Aaron during that very night, and said to them: "Arise, go out from among my people, both you and the children of Israel; and go, serve the Lord as you have said; and take your flocks and your herds, as you have said, and go, and bless me also." At last, then, the pride of the stubborn king was broken. Meanwhile the Hebrews had been preparing for their hasty departure. With beating hearts, they had assembled in groups to eat the Paschal lamb before midnight, arrayed as they had been commanded. The women had taken from the ovens the unleavened cakes, which were eaten with the meat of the roasted lamb. The preparations were at last concluded, and all was ready. At the word of command, the whole nation of the Hebrews poured forth into the cool, still Eastern morning. But not even amidst their trepidation and danger did they forget the pledge given by their ancestors to Joseph, and they carried his remains, with them, to inter them later in the Promised Land.

TEST YOUR KNOWLEDGE

1. When did the enslavement of the children of Israel in Egypt begin? (p. 83)
2. Were all the children of Israel enslaved? (p. 84)
3. How did Moses become tongue-tied? (p. 86)
4. Why did Moses flee from Egypt?
5. Was Moses a champion of the oppressed also where other than his own brethren were concerned? (p. 91)
6. Can you describe G-d's first revelation to Moses? (p. 92)
7. How old was Moses when he came to Pharaoh with his Divine mission? (p. 94)
8. Was Moses' mission a success from the start? (p. 95)
9. Why did it require faith and courage for the children of Israel to offer the Paschal sacrifice? (p. 101)
10. What finally broke Pharaoh's resistance? (p. 101)

V. A FREE NATION IN THE MAKING

33. THE EXODUS FROM EGYPT

ISRAEL LEAVES EGYPT: Thus the children of Israel were liberated from the yoke of their oppressors on the fifteenth day of Nissan in the year 2448 after the creation of the world. There were 600,000 men over 20 years of age, with their wives and children, and flocks, crossing the border of Egypt that day —a free nation. Many Egyptians and other non-Israelites joined the triumphant children of Israel, hoping to share their glorious future. The children of Israel did not leave Egypt destitute. In addition to their own possessions, the terrified Egyptians had bestowed upon them gifts of gold and silver, and clothing, in an effort to hasten their departure. Thus G-d made His promise to Abraham, that his descendants would leave their exile with great riches, come true in every detail.

Leading the Jewish people on their journey during the day was a pillar of cloud, and at night there was a pillar of fire, giving them light. These Divine messengers not only guided the children of Israel on their way, but also cleared the way before them, making it both easy and safe.

IN HOT PURSUIT: The shortest route for the children of Israel to the Promised Land, would have been straight across the land of the Philistines. However, G-d wanted to give the newly-born Jewish nation the opportunity to throw off the remnants of Egyptian influence, and to educate them in the new ways of a holy life, through the Divine Torah which was to be given to them on Mount Sinai. Furthermore, the shortest way to the Holy Land would have involved the people in a war with the Philistines, and it was doubtful whether the children of Israel, who had just left centuries of continuous slavery behind, would be strong enough to fight like free men; they might decide to return to Egypt rather than face a bloody war. Therefore, G-d led the Jewish people in a round-about way. Instead of following the coast of the Mediterranean Sea all the way to the Promised Land, they were led southwards through the desert.

After three days, Pharaoh received word of the progress of the children of Israel. The unexpected direction of their march made him think that they had gotten lost in the desert. Pharaoh now regretted that he had permitted them to leave. He immediately mobilized his army and personally took the lead of his choicest cavalry and war-chariots in hot pursuit of his former slaves. He reached them near the banks of the Red Sea, and pressed them close to the water, in an effort to cut off their escape.

Fear gripped the children of Israel as they saw the pursuing hosts of their enslavers. Some groups among them were ready to fight the Egyptians; others preferred to drown in the floods of the sea than risk defeat and return to slavery. A third group of frightened and feeble people began to complain against Moses, fearing that he had lured them out of the safety of Egypt to die in the desert. "Because there were no graves in Egypt," they exclaimed, "hast thou taken us away to die in the wilderness? Wherefore hast thou done this to us, to lead us forh out of Egypt? Is not this the word that we spoke to thee in Egypt, saying, 'Let us alone, that we may serve the Egyptians? For it is better for us to serve the Egyptians than that we should die in the wilderness.' " But Moses, calm and firm in one of the most trying moments of his life, said: "Fear ye not, stand still and see the salvation of the Lord, which He will show you today: for as you have seen the Egyptians today, you shall see them again no more forever. The Lord will fight for you, and you shall keep yourselves quiet."

Then Moses led the Israelites onwards until they came to the very borders of the Red Sea. The pillar of cloud now changed its position; for, retreating from the front to the rear of the Hebrew hosts, it floated between the two armies; over the Israelies it shed a brilliant light, while it spread a veil of darkness over the Egyptians. But the Israelites seemed now helplessly hemmed in by overwhelming dangers: the Egyptians were close behind them, and the waves of the Red Sea were breaking at their feet.

THE MIRACLE OF THE RED SEA: Then G-d spoke to Moses: "Lift thou up thy rod, and stretch out thy hand over the sea and divide it; and the children of Israel shall go into the midst of the sea on dry ground." Moses did as G-d ordered him. He raised his staff, and stretched his hand over the sea; a strong east wind rose and blew the whole night. The waters of the Red Sea were immediately divided and gathered into a wall on either side, leaving a dry passage in the midst. The Israelites marched at once along that dry path which extended from shore to shore, and gained the opposite side in safety.

THE END OF THE EGYPTIAN ARMY: The Egyptians continued their pursuit, without hesitation, in the same track. But the wheels of their chariots became clogged in the bed of the sea, and glided off. They were unable to proceed; and they felt that they were once more vainly struggling against the Lord. They turned to flee, but it was too late; for at the command of G-d, Moses stretched forth his staff, and the waters resumed their usual course, closing over the chariots and horses and warriors, over the whole host of Pharaoh. "There remained not so much as one of them."

Thus G-d saved the children of Israel from the Egyptians on that day. Israel saw His great power; they recognized G-d and believed in Him and in His servant Moses.

ISRAEL'S SONG OF PRAISE: Then Moses and the entire congregation sang this Song of Praise to G-d for their miraculous rescue.

1. *"I will sing unto the Lord, for He is highly exalted;*
   The horse and its rider hath He thrown into the sea.

2. *The Lord is my strength and song,*
   And He is become my salvation;
   This is my G-d, and I will glorify Him;
   My father's G-d, and I will exalt Him.

3. *The Lord is the lord of war,*
   The Lord is His name.

4. *Pharaoh's chariots and his host*
   hath He cast into the sea.
   And his chosen captains are sunk
   in the Red Sea.

5. *The deeps cover them—*
   they went down into the depths
   like a stone.

6. *Thy right hand, O Lord, is glorious in power,*
   Thy right hand, O Lord, dasheth
   in pieces the enemy.

7. *And in the greatness of Thine excellency*
   Thou overthrowest them that rise up against Thee;
   Thou sendest forth Thy wrath; it consumeth them
   as stubble.

8 *And with the blast of Thy nostrils*
   the waters were piled up—
   The floods stood upright as a heap;
   The deeps were congealed in the heart
   of the sea.

9. *The enemy said:*
   'I will pursue, I will overtake, I will
   divide the spoil;
   My lust shall be satisfied upon them;
   I will draw my sword, my hand shall
   destroy them.'

10. *Thou didst blow Thy wind,*
    the sea covered them.
    They sank as lead in the mighty waters.

11. *Who is like unto Thee, O Lord,*
    among the mighty?
    Who is like unto Thee, glorious in holiness,
    Fearful in praises, doing wonders?

12. *Thou stretchedst out Thy right hand—*
    The earth swallowed them.

13. *Thou in Thy love hast led the people*
    that Thou hast redeemed;
    Thou hast guided them in Thy strength
    to Thy holy habitation.

14. *The peoples have heard, they trembled;*
    Pangs have taken hold on the inhabitants
    of Philistia.

15. *Then were the chiefs of Edom*
    affrighted;
    The mighty men of Moab, trembling
    taketh hold upon them;
    All the inhabitants of Canaan are melted
    away.
16. *Terror and dread falleth upon them.*
    By the greatness of Thine arm they are
    as still as a stone;
    Till Thy people pass over, O Lord,
    Till the people pass over that Thou hast
    gotten.
17. *Thou bringest them in, and plantest them*
    in the mountain of Thine inheritance.
    The place, O Lord, which Thou hast
    made for Thee to dwell in,
    The sanctuary, O Lord, which Thy
    hands have established.
18. *The Lord shall reign for ever and ever."*

As the last words of the song died away, Miriam seized her timbrel, and followed by a multitude of Hebrew maidens and women, went forth in procession danc-and proclaiming:

"Sing ye to the Lord, for He is gloriously exalted;
The horse and its rider has He thrown into the sea."

34. FOOD IN THE DESERT

MOSES SWEETENS BITTER WATER: Leaving the shores of the Red Sea behind, the children of Israel entered the dreary wilderness of Shur, and proceeding through a pathless waste, found no springs or wells, so that they were parched with thirst. At last they arrived at a spring; but when they put their lips to the fount, they, who had so long been accustomed to the delicious and far-famed water of the Nile, found it utterly unpalatable. It was bitter and brackish, and has caused the place to be called Marah, that is, *Bitterness.* Fevered with thirst, the unfortunate people murmured against Moses, exclaiming, "What shall we drink?" Moses prayed to the Lord, and in answer to his supplications, the Lord showed him a tree, and bade him cast some of its wood into the water. No sooner was this done than the bitterness was changed into sweetness, and the Israelites were saved from the agony of thirst.

There, in Marah, G-d gave the Jewish people certain laws and commands, and told them that if they would obey G-d, nothing like what had happened to the Egyptians could happen to them. For G-d Himself would take care of them, and heal all their wounds.

MEAT AND BREAD IN THE DESERT: Weary and hungry, Israel reached the desert of Zin, and again they began to raise their voices against Moses and Aaron for leading them into a place where there was neither bread nor meat to still their hunger. They said: "Would that we had died by the hand of the Lord in the land of Egypt, when we sat by the flesh-pots, when we did eat bread to the full; for ye have brought us forth into this land to kill this whole assembly with hunger."

Thereupon G-d told Moses that He would give the children of Israel a heavenly food, that would rain down from the skies. This the children of Israel would gather every morning in an amount sufficient for a full day's needs. Only on Friday they were to gather a two days' supply, so that they would not have to go out and gather food on the Sabbath. And G-d had Moses and Aaron tell the children of Israel: "At dusk ye shall eat flesh, and in the morning ye shall be filled with bread; and ye shall know that I am the Lord your G-d." Thus it happened.

In the evening, quails came and covered the camp, so that everyone had more meat than he could possibly eat. In the morning, however, fine grains, like dew, covered the ground. The people of Israel asked what it was (Heb. *Man-hu?*). Moses replied that it was the heavenly bread G-d had given them to eat. Everyone was to gather as much as he needed for the day, but no more. Nothing was to be left for the next morning, for it would come down daily. The children of Israel called this bread from heaven "Manna." It was pure white food and tasted like the finest and most delicious foods imaginable: Whatever taste one desired, the manna had. They gathered the manna, some more, some less. But when they measured what they had, they found that nobody had more or less than he needed.

Some men, however, disobeyed Moses' order and kept some of the manna for the next day. But in the morning it had become rotten and inedible. On the sixth day, the children of Israel gathered a double portion, one for Friday and one for the Sabbath. They prepared all the food for the seventh day in advance. Only on the Sabbath day the manna gathered on the previous morning was not spoiled. On the Sabbath morning some people went out to gather manna, in defiance of Moses' order; but they did not find anything. Moses became angry at this disobedience and he told these unruly people in the name of G-d: "How long refuse ye to keep My commandments and My laws? See that the Lord hath given you the Sabbath; therefore, he giveth you on the sixth day the bread of two days; abide

ye every man in his place, let no man go out of his place
on the seventh day." Thereafter the children of Israel
rested on the seventh day, the Sabbath.

For forty years G-d fed the Jewish people this heavenly bread. At G-d's command Aaron filled one jar with
manna and kept it in the holy Tabernacle, so that the
generations to come would be able to see with their own
eyes what G-d had given to the children of Israel in the
desert after he had taken them out of Egypt.*

**WATER FROM
A ROCK:** From the desert of Zin, the Jewish
people made their way to Rephidim, another waterless place in the desert. Again
they grumbled against their leaders for leading them
through places where they and their flocks were in danger
of death through thirst. G-d ordered Moses to take the
Elders of the people to a rock which he was to hit with
his staff. From the dry stone, a well would then spring
forth, giving ample water to quench the thirst of the children of Israel, and their livestock. Moses did as G-d
had commanded him, and once again man and beast were
saved. The place where this happened afterwards was
called "Massa" (trial), and "Meriva" (strife), in commemoration of the lack of faith in G-d and Moses, which
the children of Israel had displayed in that place.

35. AMALEK'S ATTACK

**THE DEFEAT OF
AMALEK:** While the Jews were still in Rephidim, the Amalekites, a mightly and
fierce people, descendants of Esau, and
well-trained in the art of warfare, suddenly attacked the

---

* Many years later, when the Jews lacked faith in G-d, the Prophet
Jeremiah brought out the jar of manna and showed them how miraculously
G-d sustained the entire people.

people of Israel. It was an unprovoked and cowardly attack upon a tired and weary people, just liberated from slavery, on the way to their homeland.

Moses put his disciple Joshua in charge of the troops who were to fight against the Amalekites. Then Moses, together with his brother Aaron and nephew Hur, went up to a hill, to pray for G-d's help in the battle. The battle lasted a whole day until the Amalekites were finally defeated and routed. G-d ordered Moses to record the treacherous attack of the Amalekites for everlasting memory. Together with this memory went an oath to wipe the Amalekites—the incarnation of all evil—off the face of the earth. There could be no peace between Israel and Amalek for all time to come.

36. JETHRO'S VISIT AND ADVICE

JETHRO'S VISIT: At that time, Jethro, Moses' father-in-law, heard of the miracles G-d had wrought for the children of Israel, and he decided to visit Moses in the desert. He took his daughter Zipporah and her two sons, Gershom and Eliezer, and brought them to Moses. Having been informed by Jethro that he was coming and bringing with him Moses' wife and children, Moses, accompanied by the entire community of Israel, went out to greet them. Jethro, a man of great experience and much knowledge, was very much impressed by Moses' account of the historic events that had occurred to the children of Israel.

COURTS OF JUSTICE: Jethro was likewise impressed by the law and order that prevailed in the camp of Israel, though they had been mere slaves a little while before. However, he criticised Moses for taking upon himself the entire burden of dispensing justice in all matters of argument and dispute that arose in the large community of the children of Israel, number-ing several million souls. He suggested that Moses insti-tute a system of judicial organization, wherein there were to be smaller and larger courts. There were to be appointed judges and officers of different rank—officers of a thou-sand, officers of 100, of 50, and of 10. They were to shoulder the burden of straightening out all major and minor disputes of the children of Israel. Only matters of far-reaching importance were to come before Moses him-self. This suggestion of Jethro was well taken, and im-mediately put into effect.

Jethro did not stay long with Moses and the children of Israel. He returned to Midian to preach about the greatness of the G-d of Israel among the heathens. His descendants, the Kainites, remained friendly towards the Jewish people for many centuries.

37. THE REVELATION ON MOUNT SINAI

THE PREP-ARATIONS: On Rosh Chodesh Sivan, the first day of the third month after the exodus from Egypt, the children of Israel reached the desert of Sinai and camped near the mountain. During the few weeks of travelling in the desert under Divine protection, with daily miracles, such as the manna and the quail, the miraculous sweetening of the water, the de-feat of Amalek, and the crossing of the Red Sea, the Jew-ish people had become more and more conscious of G-d. Their faith grew more intense daily, until they attained a standard of holiness, solidarity, and unity, never achieved before or after by any other nation.

Moses ascended Mount Sinai, and G-d spoke to him

the following words: "Thus shalt thou say to the house of
Jacob, and tell the children of Israel: 'Ye have seen what
I did unto the Egyptians, and how I bore you on eagles'
wings, and brought you unto Myself. Now, therefore, if
ye will hearken unto My voice indeed, and keep My
covenant, then ye shall be Mine own treasure from among
all peoples; for all the earth is Mine; and ye shall be unto
Me a kingdom of priests, and a holy nation.' "

Moses returned from Sinai and called for the elders
of the people and put all these words of G-d before them.
Unanimously, with one voice and one mind, the people
answered: *Naaseh Venishma* — "Everything G-d has said,
we shall do." Thus they accepted the Torah outright, with
all its precepts, not even asking for a detailed enumeration
of the obligations and duties it involved. When Israel
had voiced its eagerness to receive the Torah, G-d spoke to
Moses again: "Go unto the people, and sanctify them
today and tomorrow, and let them wash their garments,
and be ready against the third day; for on the third day
the Lord will come down in the sight of all the people
upon Mount Sinai. And thou shalt set bounds unto the
people round about saying: Take heed to yourselves, that
ye go not up onto the Mount, or touch the border of it;
whatsoever toucheth the Mount shall surely die."

**THE REVELATION
ON SINAI:**
The dawn of the third day broke
amid thunder and lightning that filled
the air. Heavy clouds hung over the
mountain, and steadily growing sounds of the Shofar
made the people shake and tremble with fear. Moses led
the children of Israel out of the camp and placed them
at the foot of Mount Sinai, which was all covered by
smoke and was quaking, for G-d had descended upon it
in fire.

MOUNT SINAI

THE TEN COM-MANDMENTS: The sound of the Shofar grew louder, but suddenly all sounds ceased, and an absolute silence ensued; and then G-d proclaimed the Ten Commandments as follows:

1. *"I am the Lord thy G-d, Who brought thee out of the land of Egypt, out of the house of bondage.*

2. *"Thou shalt have no other gods before Me. Thou shalt not make unto thee a graven image, nor any manner of likeness, of any thing that is in heaven above, or that is in the earth beneath, or that is in the water under the earth; thou shalt not bow down unto them, nor serve them; for I the Lord thy G-d am a jealous G-d, visiting the iniquity of the fathers upon the children of the third and fourth generation of them that hate Me; and showing mercy unto the thousandth generation of them that love Me and keep My commandments.*

3. *"Thou shalt not take the name of the Lord thy G-d in vain; for the Lord will not hold him guiltless that taketh His name in vain.*

4. *"Remember the Sabbath Day, to keep it holy. Six days shalt thou labor, and do all thy work; but the seventh day is a Sabbath unto the Lord thy G-d, in it thou shalt not do any manner of work, thou, nor thy son, nor thy daughter, nor thy man-servant, nor thy maid-servant, nor thy cattle, nor thy stranger that is within thy gates; for in six days the Lord made heaven and earth, the sea and all that in them is, and rested on the seventh day; wherefore the Lord blessed the Sabbath Day, and hallowed it.*

5. *"Honor thy father and thy mother, that thy days may be long upon the land which the Lord thy G-d giveth thee.*

6. *"Thou shalt not murder.*

7. *"Thou shalt not commit adultery.*

8. *"Thou shalt not steal.*

9. *"Thou shalt not bear false witness against thy neighbor.*

10. *"Thou shalt not covet thy neighbor's house; thou shalt not covet thy neighbor's wife, nor his man-servant, nor his maid-servant, nor his ox, nor his ass, nor anything that is thy neighbor's."*

MOSES RECEIVES THE TORAH: The entire people heard the words of G-d, and they became frightened. They begged Moses to be the intermediary between G-d and them, for if G-d Himself would continue to give them the entire Torah, they would surely die. Moses told them not to be afraid, for G-d had revealed Himself to them so that they would fear Him and not sin.

Then G-d asked Moses to ascend the mountain; for he alone was able to stand in the presence of G-d. There Moses was to receive the two tablets containing the Ten Commandments, and the entire Torah, to teach it to the children of Israel. Moses went up the mountain and stayed there forty days and forty nights, without food or sleep, for he had become like an angel. During this time, G-d revealed to Moses the entire Torah, with all its laws and the interpretations thereof. Finally, G-d gave Moses the two stone Tables of Testimony, containing the Ten Commandments, written by G-d Himself.

38. THE GOLDEN CALF

REBELLION: Moses had promised the children of Israel that he would return after forty days. The fortieth day had arrived and the people became anxious and nervous. During Moses' long absence, the Egyptian riff-raff that had accompanied the children of Israel since their exodus from Egypt, spread the word around that Moses would never return and that they had better choose another leader to be the intermediary between them and G-d. The children of Israel did not realize that Moses had meant that he would return after the *completion* of forty full days. Therefore, when the sixteenth of Tammuz, which was the fortieth day since the Revelation, arrived, and Moses had not returned, they stormed against Aaron and Hur, Miriam's son, who had temporarily taken over the leadership of the Jewish camp, demanding that they make an idol to take Moses' place. In vain did Hur try to talk the excited group of ringleaders out of their plan. His persistent refusal to go ahead with it enraged them so much that they killed him. Now Aaron saw that there was little chance of stopping them. He would only share a similar fate, and the people would have committed the indelible crime of having murdered their own High Priest.

AARON PLAYS FOR TIME: Aaron knew that Moses would return the next morning. He therefore decided to play for time. He asked everyone to bring his own and his wife's gold and jewelry for the purpose of making the idol. Thus, he thought, he would delay the whole affair, since he expected that the people would refuse to part with their precious jewelry and ornaments. But contrary to his expectations, the mob willingly parted with their gold, though the women did refuse to be a party to it. Aaron had no other choice but to take the heap of golden rings, chains, and bracelets that had been piled up before him and throw it into the melting-pot. Applying their knowledge of magic, the Egyptian conspirators made the gold assume the form of a calf.

When the children of Israel saw it, they believed that it was to be their representative before G-d, and they wanted to pay homage to it. But Aaron made another desperate effort to delay the idolatry. He told the people that on the next day he would build an altar, and proclaim a special day of worship.

Meanwhile, G-d informed Moses of the downfall of the children of Israel, and of the severe punishment that awaited them. They would die, and a new people, descendants of Moses, would take their places, to carry the torch of the Divine Law among the nations of the world.

Moses was greatly distressed. In moving words, he prayed and implored G-d to spare the Jewish people. Moses recalled G-d's covenant with Abraham, Isaac, and Jacob, and for their sake begged G-d's forgiveness. Finally, G-d's mercy was aroused, and He promised to spare the people of Israel.

MOSES' RETURN: Assured of G-d's forgiveness, Moses descended from Mount Sinai. Exactly forty days had passed since he had gone up, and in his hands he carried the Tables of Testimony, written by G-d Himself. At the foot of the mountain his disciple Joshua awaited him, and together they approached the camp of Israel. When they came within hearing distance of the camp, shouts of jubilation and joy reached their ears. Moses soon saw what was going on. In despair, he threw the Tables of Testimony to the ground, shattering them into small pieces. A people who could worship a golden calf so soon after they faced G-d and heard His voice say, "Thou shalt not make thee a graven image," did not deserve this treasure, Moses thought. Then he took the golden idol, ground it to dust and spread the dust over the water, which he made the people drink. Thus he showed them the impotence of their idol, and the foolishness of their action.

PUNISHMENT OF THE GUILTY: Taking up a position near the entrance of the camp, Moses said: "Whoever is with G-d, come to me!" The entire tribe of Levi gathered about him, and Moses ordered them to slay every one guilty of worshipping the Golden Calf, regardless of his position and relationship to them. That day, the seventeenth day of Tammuz, three thousand men of the children of Israel lost their lives, in punishment for their idolatry.

ATONEMENT: The next day Moses again told the people that they had gravely sinned against G-d, and that he would now go to pray for atonement. Moses went up to Mount Sinai, and prayed to G-d for forty days and forty nights, while the people mourned their dead, and made atonement for their sin.

SECOND TABLES: After Moses had descended from Mount Sinai, G-d told him to hew another pair of tables, similar to the one he had received the first time. Moses was then to ascend Mount Sinai for the third time, when G-d would inscribe upon them the Ten Commandments, as He had done before.

On the first day of Elul, Moses went up to Mount Sinai and stayed with G-d for the third time, for forty days and forty nights, neither eating nor sleeping. G-d inscribed the Ten Commandments on the tables and told Moses He forgave the children of Israel.

G-D FORGIVES THE PEOPLE: Holding the newly hewn tables in his hands, Moses stood on Mount Sinai and G-d taught him how the children of Israel could make atonement for their sins through real re-

pentance and prayer. Thereupon G-d proclaimed the
"thirteen attributes" which the children of Israel were to
recite on their days of repentance: "The Lord, the Lord,
G-d, merciful and gracious, long-suffering, and abundant
in goodness and truth; keeping mercy unto the thousandth
generation, forgiving iniquity, and transgression and sin,
who will by no means clear the guilty; visiting the iniquity of the fathers upon the children, and upon the children's children, unto the third and unto the fourth generation."

Moses bowed down before G-d and said: "If now
I have found grace in Thy sight, O Lord, let the Lord, I
pray Thee, go in the midst of us; for it is a stiff-necked
people; and pardon our iniquity and our sin, and take us
for Thine inheritance."

In reply, G-d told Moses: "Behold, I make a convenant; before all thy people I will do marvels, such as have
not been wrought in all the earth, nor in any nation; and
all the people among which thou art shall see the work of
the Lord that I am about to do with thee, that it is
tremendous."

It was the tenth day of Tishrei (Yom Kippur) when
Moses returned to the camp of Israel, with the new Tables
of Testimony in his hands. Moses' face shone with a Divine light that frightened Aaron and the children of Israel. They drew back in awe when Moses approached
them. On learning of this, Moses covered his face with a
veil. Without delay, he proceeded to teach the children of
Israel the entire contents of the Torah which G-d had
given him on Mount Sinai.

39. THE PEOPLE OF THE BOOK

THE STUDY OF THE TORAH: The manner in which Moses taught the Torah to the people was as follows: After Moses received the precept from G-d, he taught it to Aaron; then, in Aaron's presence, to Aaron's sons; then again, in the presence of Aaron and his sons, to the Seventy Elders of Israel; finally, in the presence of all these disciples, to the whole people of Israel. Moses having left, the entire procedure was repeated, with Aaron being the teacher. After Aaron finished, his sons served as teachers; finally the Elders took over, repeating the precept to the people for the fourth time.

The result of this intensive study was that each party studied the Torah four times outright, and thus it was fully and permanently retained in the memory of both the leaders and the people.

At the end of the forty years' wandering in the desert, five weeks before his death, Moses repeated the Torah to the children of ısrael for the last time, and once again explained it to them thoroughly. He wrote it down in the "Five Books of Moses," as dictated to him by G-d. The Torah was written down in thirteen copies, one for each tribe and one to be placed in the Holy Ark in the Sanctuary. (See *chapter* 40).

613 PRECEPTS: The Torah contains 613 commandments. Of these, 248 are "positive" commands (do's), and 365 are "negative" commands (don'ts).

The precepts form the code of the Jew's daily behavior and his way of life. They help him lead an honest, clean, and healthful life, both in body and in spirit.

The precepts are generally divided into two groups:

The Jew's duties toward his fellow man, and his duties toward his Creator, G-d.

The former, that is the duties of the Jew towards his fellow man, include all those laws of honesty, uprightness, truthfulness, kindness, and charitableness, which he is to practise in all his dealings. By observing these precepts, the Jew attains the highest perfection as a human being and as a member of a most perfect state of family and social life. These laws form the bulk of the precepts of the Torah.

The other group, that is the laws concerning the Jew's duties toward his Maker, include the laws of worship, festivals, diet (Kashruth), and many other laws designed to enable him to attain the highest form of spiritual life.

THE HEBREW CALENDAR: The Torah fixes the Jewish week of six working days and one day of rest on Saturday—which is the Holy Shabbos. All manner of work, and even certain weekday pleasures, are forbidden on Shabbos, as this day is to be entirely devoted to spiritual life—to the study of the Torah and to prayer.

The Hebrew months consists of twenty-nine or thirty days. It is a "Lunar" month (based on the moon), contrary to most non-Jewish calendars which are based on the sun and therefore called "Solar."

The first month is *Nissan,* the month of the spring, in which the children of Israel were liberated from Egypt. But the Jewish New Year is at the beginning of *Tishrei* (the seventh month), since the world was created at that time, according to Jewish tradition.

THE FESTIVALS: The principal Jewish festivals are *Rosh Hashanah* (New Year), which takes place on the first and second of Tishrei, and *Yom*

"THREE TIMES IN THE YEAR"
(*The Three Festivals*)

Kippur (Day of Atonement), which is on the tenth of Tishrei. The other major festivals are the "Three Festivals" (*Shalosh Regalim*): Passover (*Pesach*)—on the 15th of Nissan (eight days); The Feast of Weeks (*Shovuoth*)—on the 6th and 7th of Sivan, and the Feast of Tabernacles (*Succoth*)—on the 15th of Tishrei (nine days). These three festivals commemorate the most important events in Jewish history: the liberation from Egypt (Pesach), the giving of the Torah (Shovuoth), and the forty years' wandering of the Jews in the desert (Succoth).

In later years, two more festivals were added to the Jewish calendar—Purim and Chanukah, and four *fasts* connected with the destruction of the Holy Temple in Jerusalem and the exile of the Jewish people from the Land of Israel. More will be said about these events later.

A HOLY NATION: At the time the Torah was given to the people of Israel more than 32 centuries ago, (2448 years, or 26 generations, after the creation of the world), and for many centuries afterwards, most peoples of the earth lived in a state of lawlessness, violence, and immorality. At Sinai Israel was designated by G-d to be "a kingdom of priests and a holy nation," to teach the world the truth about the Creator and the way He wants the human race to live upon this earth. At Mount Sinai the Jewish people solemnly undertook to adhere to the Torah and to its precepts at all times and in all places, so that they would indeed be a living symbol of a Divinely inspired people. In accordance with this solemn covenant between G-d and Israel, reaffirmed many times in the Torah, the destiny and fate of the Jewish people would be determined by their faith in G-d and their loyalty to the precepts of the Torah. The Jewish people were thus made the torch-bearers of Divine wisdom in the world, until the great day when "all the earth shall be filled with the knowledge of G-d as the waters fill the ocean."

40. THE TABERNACLE

THE SANCTUARY: On the day after Moses returned from Mt. Sinai with the Second Tables, he gathered about him the entire congregation of Israel, and told them that G-d had ordered them to build a place of worship, or a Tabernacle, which was to be a visible emblem of G-d's presence in the midst of Israel. "They shall make Me a sanctuary; and I will dwell in their midst," were G-d's words. For this purpose G-d had asked them for voluntary contributions of gold, silver, copper, precious stones, wool, and linen.

When the people heard the good news, they gave freely of everything useful and precious that they owned; the women also spun and wove artistic handicraft. The princes contributed precious stones, fine oil, and rare spices. Day after day the entire community brought rich gifts as their offerings to G-d's sanctuary, until the contributions were more than was necessary for the construction of the Tabernacle and its furnishings. Moses had to stop the ceaseless flow of contributions.

THE ARCHITECTS: Two men, Bezalel and Oholiav, who were gifted with Divine wisdom and artistic knowledge, were appointed to take charge of the construction of the Tabernacle. They, and with them all those who had any knowledge of art and beauty, wrought and perfected the parts of the holy Tabernacle and its furnishings, according to the picture and plan G-d had shown to Moses on the mountain.

PLAN OF THE SANCTUARY: The Tabernacle consisted of a tent that could be taken apart and moved from place to place. An artistically woven curtain, (the *Porocheth*) embroidered with *cherubim*, which was held up by four wooden pillars overlaid with gold, separated the tent into two chambers: The front chamber was called the *Holy Place*, and the inner chamber was called the *Holy of Holies*.

The walls of the sanctuary were made of wooden boards which rested in silver sockets, and which were overlaid with a fine cover of gold. The roof and outer walls were covered with expensive carpets and skins. Before the entrance into the sanctuary there hung an artistically woven curtain. The tent of the Tabernacle stood in a wide court, enclosed by curtains supported by pillars.

THE HOLY VESSELS: On the south side of the Court, facing the entrance, stood the *Altar of Burnt-Sacrifice*, made of Shittim-wood, covered with copper. Behind the altar, that is, between the altar and the Tabernacle, stood the Laver of brass, at which the priests had to wash before entering the sanctuary proper.

In the Tabernacle, on its northern side, stood the *Table*, made of Shittim-wood, but overlaid with pure gold, and with a crown of gold all around it. On this table lay twelve loaves of unleavened bread, (the "Show-Bread"), which were replaced every Sabbath by fresh ones. In the south, stood the *Candlestick*, hammered out of pure gold, richly decorated and ornamented with flowerbuds, blossoms, and petals; its seven lamps were lighted every evening. In the middle of the room was the *Altar of Incense*, made of Shittim-wood and overlaid with gold. On it, the finest spices were offered to G-d, every day, morning and evening.

The two Tables of Testimony, which Moses had brought back from Mount Sinai were kept in the *Ark* of Shittim-wood. The Ark was overlaid with pure gold from within and from without. The Holy Ark stood in the Holy of Holies. Its lid was made of pure gold, and out of it were beaten two *Cherubim*, spreading forth their wings, with their faces turned toward each other. Golden rings were attached to the corners of the Ark so that it could be carried on poles when the camp was on the move.

THE PRIESTS: G-d selecterd Aaron and his four sons, Nadab, Abihu, Elazar, and Ithamar, as priests to serve in the Tabernacle, on behalf of the entire Jewish people. The first-born who originally had been destined to be the priests of G-d, had lost this privilege as a consequence of the sin of the Golden Calf, of which sin the entire tribe of Levy was free. Therefore, G-d selected the tribe of Levy and sanctified it to serve Him in the Sanctuary.

The vestments of the common priests consisted of a white linen tunic, trousers, girdle, and a white turban.

The High-Priest shared these garments with the common priests; but he had, besides, other vestments and ornaments which proclaimed his office to be one of higher importance and holiness. These included the plate of pure gold ("*Tzitz*") which he wore on his brow and which extended right across his forehead. It was held in place by a thread of blue. On this glittering ornament the words, "Holiness to the Lord" were inscribed. They declared that the wearer was entirely devoted to the service of G-d.

His most characteristic garment was the *Ephod*, which he wore above the tunic. It was made of the finest texture, not only of blue and crimson fine twined linen, but also of gold threads. It was caught on the shoulders by two onyx-stones set in gold. On these onyx-stones the names of the twelve tribes of Israel were engraved, six on each stone, according to their age; and the High-Priest wore these stones as "stones of memorial" for the children of Israel when he stood before G-d.

Attached to the Ephod, by two chains of gold and resting upon the heart, was the *Breast-plate of Decision.* On the breast-plate sparkled twelve precious stones in four equal rows; and in the stones the names of the twelve tribes of Israel were engraved. There the *Urim and Thummim* were placed, which the Hight-priest consulted on important matters, such as whether or not to declare war, and other questions which concerned the welfare of the whole people. On these occasions, the stones would light up and form words which revealed the answers to the questions.

To complete his attire, the High-priest wore between the Ephod and the tunic—the *Robe,* which was of fine blue wool, and which ended in a broad hem of pomegranates of blue, red, and crimson. Between these small pomegranates small golden bells were inserted, the sound of which, when Aaron walked into the Sanctuary, was to impress the minds of the Israelites with deep reverence.

Thus magnificently were the High-priest and the priests attired; yet were they to approach the Sanctuary with uncovered feet, that they might constanly be reminded of modesty and humility.

Aaron and his sons had to take care of the offerings to G-d and to bless the children of Israel with the words: *"The Lord bless thee, and keep thee: the Lord make His face to shine upon thee, and be gracious unto thee; the Lord turn His face unto thee, and give thee peace."*

The rest of the work in the Holy Tabernacle was given over to the members of the other families of Levi.

CONSECRATION OF THE TABERNACLE: After the various parts and vessels of the Sanctuary had been finished, Moses set up the Holy Tabernacle and placed each vessel in accordance with G-d's command. Then he arranged a seven-day period for the consecration of the sanctuary and installation of the priests in their holy offices.

On the first day of Nissan of the second year after the exodus from Egypt, the erection of the Holy Tabernacle was completed. When Aaron placed the first sacrifice on the altar, G-d sent a flame of fire which devoured the pieces of meat on the altar. The entire people had watched with awe this sign of G-d's presence in the Tabernacle and worshipped Him, joyously bowing down before His Divine Majesty.

DEATH OF NADAB AND ABIHU: On the same day, the princes of the twelve tribes, began to bring their dedication offerings. Yet the happiness of the day was marred by a very sad incident. Nadab and Abihu had become so inspired and intoxicated with the joy of their holy task as priests to G-d, that they wanted to do more than G-d had commanded them. They offered incense on the altar, burning it on unconsecrated fire. Suddenly, a flame of fire shot forth from heaven, killing them both. Crushed with grief over the loss of his two eldest sons, but realizing that it was a Divine punishment, Aaron kept silent. The sanctity of the Tabernacle now became even more evident than before.

THE PILLARS OF CLOUD AND FIRE: During the day, the Holy Tabernacle was always covered by a pillar of cloud, and in the night by a pillar of fire. As long as the pillar of cloud rested over the Tabernacle, the children of Israel remained in the same place. When the cloud rose up, it was a sign for them to continue their journey. Thus they camped and travelled according to G-d's command.

When the Holy Ark, containing the Tables of Testimony, was raised upon the shoulders of its carriers, Moses said: "Rise up, O G-d, and let Thine enemies be scattered; and let them that hate Thee flee before Thee." When the Ark was let down to rest, Moses exclaimed: "Return O G-d, unto the ten thousands of the families of Israel."

In order to gain the attention of the vast multitude, whether upon the march or during the encampment, Moses was commanded to use two silver trumpets; their loud and significant blast would be a summons for the people and a "memorial" before G-d; it was to be a signal for the whole community or the chiefs to assemble before the Tabernacle, or to prepare for departure from the encampment; it led the warriors to battle, and proclaimed the holy festivals, the days of gladness and thanksgiving, of solemnity and humiliation. On each occassion there was, of course, a different signal.

TEST YOUR KNOWLEDGE

1. What was the approximate number of the children of Israel upon liberation from Egypt? (p. 103)
2. Why did they not take the shortest route to the Promised Land? (p. 104)
3. Who was the leader of the Hebrew women at that time? (p. 108)
4. What miracles did G-d perform for the liberated hosts of Israel after the crossing of the Red Sea? (pp. 109-111, e.a.)
5. Who were the Amalekites? (p. 111)
6. What is the meaning of "Massa" and "Meriva"? (p. 111)
7. What important advice of Jethro to Moses was immediately put into effect? (p. 112)
8. When was the Torah given to Israel on Mount Sinai? (pp. 113, 114)
9. What are the 4th, 5th and 10th Commandments? (pp. 117, 118)
10. Why did the children of Israel want a Golden Calf? (pp. 118, 119)
11. Was Aaron anxious to be a party to the rebellion? (p. 119)
12. What are the "Thirteen Attributes"? (p. 122)
13. How many precepts does the Torah contain? (p. 123)
14. What do you know about the Hebrew Calendar? (p. 124)
15. What is the meaning of "A kingdom of priests and a holy nation"? (p. 127)
16. Who were the architects of the Tabernacle in the desert? (p. 128)
17. Can you enumerate the holy vessels of the Tabernacle? (p. 129)
18. What were the "Tzitz" and "Ephod"? (p. 130)
19. What is the "Priestly Blessing"? (p. 131)
20. What were the "silver trumpets" used for? (p. 133)

VI. FORTY YEARS TO THE PROMISED LAND

41. TRIALS IN THE DESERT

DEPARTURE FROM SINAI: The children of Israel had camped for almost an entire year near Mount Sinai, when the pillar of cloud rose for the first time, over the Tabernacle. At once, the children of Israel resumed their journey. Marching according to the order given by G-d, the Jewish people continued their journey until they reached the Desert of Paran.

THE PEOPLE ASK FOR MEAT: The weariness of the people began to tell on them. The Egyptian riffraff that had joined them upon their liberation from Egypt, again sowed the seed of discontent among their Jewish neighbors. Soon the children of Israel began to cry over the "lost paradise" of Egypt and the privations of the desert. They complained: "Would that we were given flesh to eat! We remember the fish which we were wont to eat in Egypt for nought; the cucumbers and the melons, and the leeks, and the onions, and the garlic; but now our soul is dried away; there is nothing at all; we have nought save this manna to look to."

Moses heard this outcry with sorrow and grief, and he cried to G-d and entreated His help. The Lord listened to his prayer. He commanded him to select seventy elders, upon whom G-d would bestow His Divine spirit; they would share the burden of leading the people. G-d also promised that the people should have the flesh they were coveting, but that it should come to them as a bitter punishment: "You shall not eat one day, nor two days, nor five days, nor ten days, nor twenty days, but even a whole month, until it comes out at your nostrils, and

it is loathsome to you: because you have despised the Lord
who is among you, and have wept before Him, saying,
'Why did we come forth out of Egypt?' "

Astonished at the prospect of providing meat for such
a multitude, Moses asked where he was to get so many
animals in the desert to give meat to a people that counted
over 600,000 men, besides their wives and children?

"Shall G-d's hand be too short?" replied G-d.

Now a strong wind rose and blew flocks of quails into
the camp. They came in such multitudes that they covered
the ground two cubits high for a space of a day's journey
round the camp. The people gathered eagerly, and ate
to their full satisfaction. While they were still enjoying
that longed-for food, they were smitten by a fearful
plague, which caused death and desolation in the camp;
hence the place received the name *Kivroth-hattaavah*,
that is, Graves of Greediness.

**THE SEVENTY
ELDERS:**
The seventy elders were now selected
to ease the burden upon Moses' shoulders.
At that time an episode occurred which
reflects the character of Moses in all its purity and greatness. Two of the selected men who were to be candidates
for leadership had remained in the camp, for G-d had
asked for only seventy, whereas there were seventy-two
candidates selected from the twelve tribes, six from each.
Eldad and Medad were the two that had been eliminated
by drawing lots, but although they were not among those
congregated before the Tabernacle, G-d's spirit rested
upon them also, and they began to prophesy within the
camp stating that Moses would die before entering the
Land of Israel, and that his disciple, Joshua, would lead
the children of Israel into Canaan. Joshua, Moses' close disciple and servant, complained about them to his master.
But Moses told him: "Art thou jealous for my sake? Would

that all t   Lord's people were prophets, that the Lord would ut His spirit upon them."

MIRIAM'S SIN: As time went on, Miriam and Aaron, who, next to Moses, were the greatest leaders and prophets in Israel, felt somehow slighted by the extraordinary position of their brother, and they spoke unkindly of Moses. G-d heard their unkind words, and knowing that Moses, far from being conceited, was the most modest of living people, came to Miriam and Aaron, and told them: "Hear now My words: if there be a prophet among you, I the Lord do make Myself known unto him in a vision, I do speak with him in a dream. My servant Moses not so; he is trusted in all My house: with him do I speak mouth to mouth, even manifestly, and not in the dark speeches; wherefore then were ye not afraid to speak against My servant, against Moses?"

The next moment, Miriam discovered that she had been stricken with leprosy, and that her skin had turned as white as snow. Aaron begged Moses' forgiveness and implored him to pray to G-d to heal their sister, and Moses did so without delay. G-d heard his prayer, and told him that Miriam was to stay outside of the camp, like all other unclean people, for seven days; afterwards, she would be cured and permitted to return. Thus, Miriam was placed outside of the camp, and the entire people waited for her return to camp before continuing on their way.

42. THE SCOUTS AND THEIR EVIL REPORT

MOSES SENDS SCOUTS TO CANAAN: While the children of Israel were camping in the desert near Kadesh-Barnea, and the land of Canaan was not far away, they demanded that Moses send a group of scouts to spy out the country, so that they might be informed of its strength and weaknesses.

G-d told Moses to fulfill the people's request, whereupon, Moses selected twelve eminent men, each one a leader of his tribe, and sent them on this mission. Among them were Joshua of the tribe of Ephraim, and Caleb, Miriam's husband, of the tribe of Judah. Before they left, Moses told them "Get you up into the South, and go up into the mountains; and see the land, what it is; and the people that dwelleth therein, whether they are strong or weak, whether they are few or many; and what the land is that they dwell in, whether it is good or bad; and what cities they are that they dwell in, whether in camps or in strongholds; and what the land is, whether it is fat or lean; whether there is wood therein, or not. And be ye of good courage, and bring of the fruit of the land."

The twelve men left on their mission to spy out the land of Canaan. They crossed the entire southern part of the country till they reached Hebron, the dwelling place of giants. While in Hebron, Caleb went to the Cave of Machpelah to pray to G-d.

The scouts had become so impressed and overawed by the size and strength of the inhabitants of the land, that they decided the land was unconquerable. Only Caleb and Joshua did not lose their faith in G-d, and knew that He would keep His promise. The spies took back with them some of the choicest fruits of the country, such as figs, pomegranates, and grapes which were so heavy that eight men had to carry one cluster of grapes on two poles.

RETURN OF THE SPIES: After an absence of forty days, the twelve scouts returned to the camp at Kadesh with magnificent specimens of Canaan's produce. But the account they gave was not altogether cheering. A beautiful country, truly, said the spies, and a land that flowed with milk and honey, but a country with strong cities inhabited by formidable men, among whom was the fierce race of giants, the terrible sons of Anak. Not a province but what was occupied by warlike tribes, the Amalekites in the South, the Hittites, the Jebusites, and the Amorites in the mountain passes, and the Canaanites in the plains and on the banks of the Jordan.

The people's hearts sank within them; they felt unable to encounter such powerful foes; but Caleb, wishing to inspire them with hope and fortitude, exclaimed: "Let us go up and possess it at once; we are well able to overcome them." Alas! His cowardly companions would not hear of encouragement; they began to exaggerate the danger: "The land which we had gone to search is a land that eats up its inhabitants; and all the people that we saw in it are men of great stature. And there we saw the giants, the sons of Anak, who came of the giants; and we were in our own sight as grasshoppers, and so we were in their sight." They upbraided Moses and Aaron and proposed in their blind folly to choose a captain who might lead them back to Egypt. At night (it was the night of Tisha B'Av) the people wept in their tents, voicing their bitter complaint against Moses and Aaron for leading them into such a predicament. Now they were stuck in the desert, a prey to thirst, hunger, and wild animals. They would do better to return to the slavery of Egypt than die here.

In vain did Joshua and Caleb try to allay the excitement and despondency of the people. They pointed to the excellence of the land, and to G-d's promise, which was a better guarantee than all military power and strategy. But the people were in a mood of defiance and revolt. They would have stoned Joshua and Caleb, had G-d not saved them from their hands, by causing His cloud of glory to appear over the Sanctuary.

PENALTY FOR THE REVOLT: Then G-d declared to Moses that, as a punishment for their disbelief, the people should be smitten with pestilence and die; from Moses alone should descend a great and mighty nation, bearing G-d's name and spreading His truth. But Moses entreated G-d to forgive them. And the Lord said: "I pardon according to thy word. But as truly as I live and all the earth shall be filled with the glory of the Lord. Because all those men who have seen My glory, and My miracles which I did in Egypt and in the wilderness, have tempted Me now these ten times, and have not hearkened to My voice; surely they shall not see the land which I swore to their fathers, neither shall any of them that provoked Me see it: but My servant Caleb, because he has another spirit within him, and has followed Me fully, him will I bring into the land whereinto he went, and his seed shall posess it."

For forty years, G-d continued, the Hebrews would lead a wandering life in the desert, one year for each day spent by the spies in their journey of exploration; to their children was to be reserved the conquest of the land which they themselves dreaded so much; and of all their vast hosts, Joshua and Caleb alone, the brave-hearted and loyal followers of Moses, were to be permitted to enter the Land of Promise.

Then, all the scouts, save Joshua and Caleb, died a sudden death.

THE REBELS' SECOND DISOBEDIENCE: When Moses brought these words of G-d to the children of Israel, they mourned deeply. Finally, in their despair, they decided to make good their

sin by an immediate attack against the land of Canaan.
Moses begged them not to do anything without G-d's
orders. He warned them of certain defeat, but they persisted in their plan and marched out of camp. As Moses
had predicted, the rebellious troops of the children of Israel were vanquished by the armies of the Amalekites and
Canaanites. Those who escaped the sword returned dis-
heartened and repenting.

43. SABBATH DESECRATION AND BLASPHEMY

PUNISHMENT FOR THE DESECRATION OF SABBATH: Once, while the children of Israel
were camping in the desert, a man
by the name of Zelophehad, committed an act of public desecration,
of the Sabbath by gathering wood in front of everyone on
the Sabbath day. He was brought before Moses and put
in temporary custody, till G-d should pronounce his
penalty.

By Divine judgment he was ordered to be led outside
of the camp, and to be publicly stoned, in atonement for
his great sin. Although Zelophehad died the death of a
sinner, he called the attention of all of Israel to the holiness of the Sabbath and to the consequences of its desecration.

PUNISHMENT FOR BLASPHEMY: Among the children of Israel lived
a man whose father was an Egyptian
and whose mother was a Jewess.
Once he got into an argument, and in his lack of reverence
for G-d, blasphemed the Divine Name. He, too, was
brought before Moses and put under guard till G-d should
pronounce his punishment. Again G-d told Moses that the
blasphemer was to be brought outside the camp and stoned

in front of the entire community, as a solemn warning to all.

44. KORAH'S REBELLION

KORAH AND HIS ASSOCIATES: Korah, one of the rich leaders of the Levites, and a cousin of Moses and Aaron, felt that he had been slighted and overlooked in the distribution of the highest priestly honors and leadership. He envied Moses and Aaron, and also his cousin Elzaphan, who had been put in charge of the Levites, after Aaron's family had become elevated to the rank of Kohanim (*priests*). Realizing that despite his riches and influence he alone could do very little to shake the people's faith and confidence in Moses and Aaron, Korah looked for associates in his campaign against them.

Korah went to the people of the tribe of Reuben, his neighbors in the camping order. Being daily in close contact with them, Korah easily swayed the opinions of their leaders and drew them into his conspiracy. Amongst the Reubenites were two men, Dathan and Abiram, who since their early days in Egypt had been trouble-makers and the ringleaders of disaffection and rebellion. They were the first to rally to the party of Korah, and they were his most eager agents among their tribesmen. Their experienced and clever campaigning, aided by Korah's riches, influence, and knowledge, induced as many as 250 respected leaders of the Jewish camp to join the rebellion. They now felt bold enough to go out into the open and speak up against Moses' leadership of the people. Adopting the mantle of piety and justice, and pretending to be a champion of his people, Korah accused Moses and Aaron of imposing their leadership upon the community. "Seeing all the congregation are holy, wherefore then lift ye up yourselves above the assembly of G-d?" said Korah and his men to Moses and Aaron.

MOSES ADMONISHES THE REBELS: When Moses heard of the public accusations made against him by members of the tribe of Levi and their associates, he prayed to G-d for guidance in his new tribulation. Then he addressed himself to Korah and his party, and told them to prepare themselves for the next day, when G-d would show whom He considered worthy to serve Him as priests. All the contestants were to take censers and offer incense before G-d. G-d would then show whether He approved of this act. Moses spoke to Korah privately and warned him against his lust for personal honor. "Is it but a small thing unto you that the G-d of Israel had separated you from the congregation of Israel, to bring you near to Himself, to do the service in the Tabernacle of G-d, and to stand before the congregation to minister to them? Now will ye seek the priesthood also?" Moses said. But his words fell on deaf ears.

DATHAN'S AND ABIRAM'S SPITE After his unsuccessful talk with Korah, Moses sent for Dathan and Abiram, ringleaders of the rebellion among the non-Levites. However, they replied with their usual arrogance: "We will not come; is it a small thing that thou hast brought us out of a land flowing with milk and honey, to kill us in the wilderness, but thou must needs make thyself also a prince over us?" Moses was deeply hurt by this venomous attack upon his leadership, and he prayed to G-d to expose the wickedness of these people before the entire congregation of Israel.

PUNISHMENT OF THE REBELS: The next morning Korah's associates appeared before the Tabernacle with censers, as Moses had told them to do. With them came the entire community whom Korah had called to witness the proceedings. Then G-d told Moses to order the children of Israel to separate themselves from Korah and his associates, and everything that belonged to them, lest they share the rebels' fate. Again Moses and the Elders approached Dathan and Abiram in a last minute effort to induce them to repent of their sin. However, it was in vain, and Moses ordered the rest of the people to depart from the tents of Dathan and Abiram. The people obeyed. Dathan and Abiram and their families stood in front of their tents, and in a defiant mood continued to abuse Moses.

Gravely, Moses told the children of Israel: "Hereby ye shall know that G-d hath sent me to do all these acts, and that I have not done them of my own mind. If these men die the common death of all men . . . then G-d hath not sent me. But if G-d make a new thing, and the ground open her mouth and swallow them up with everything that belongs to them, and they go down alive unto the pit, then ye shall understand that these men have despised G-d." Hardly had Moses finished speaking, when the earth cleft asunder, and swallowed Korah and his associates with their families and belongings. They were buried alive and perished by a terrible death that made the people who stood nearby flee in terror. The next instant a fire from heaven devoured the 250 men who had dared to contest Aaron's priestly authority by offering incense.

THE BUDDING STAFF: The following day, some of the children of Israel complained that Moses and Aaron had caused the death of so many leading men, whereupon, G-d sent a plague which killed many thousands more of the rebels.

The authority of Aaron as High-priest was to be openly proved, so that his supremacy might forever be assured and recognized. Each tribe was commanded to bring one rod inscribed with its name; that of the tribe of Levi was to bear the name of Aaron. The rods were given to Moses, who took them into the Tabernacle. The tribe whose rod would blossom and bud was to be considered as especially elected and favored by G-d.

Moses did as G-d had ordered him. The next morning the priests entered the Sanctuary, and saw that Aaron's staff had budded and blossomed and yielded ripe almonds! Moses carried the rods out to the children of Israel, and each of the tribes took its rod. Everyone was now convinced of Aaron's right to the priesthood.

45. THE LAST YEAR IN THE WILDERNESS

MIRIAM'S DEATH: All through their years of wandering in the desert, a well coming out of a rock had provided the children of Israel with water. This well accompanied them wherever they went. It was a miracle with which G-d favored the children of Israel because of the merits of Miriam, Moses' sister. On the tenth day of Nissan, in the fortieth year of their journey (2487), the children of Israel reached Kadesh, in the Desert of Zin. It was there that Miriam died to the great sorrow of the Jewish people. Not only had they lost their great prophetess, but with her death, the well ceased to give them water.

THE PEOPLE GRUMBLE AGAIN: Stricken with thirst, the children of Israel again began to quarrel and murmur against Moses, saying that they would rather have died a sudden death by plague, like their brothers, than perish by thirst with their herds.

G-d told Moses to take his staff and, together with Aaron, to assemble the entire people. Then, before the eyes of all, he was to order the rock to bring forth water.

THE SIN OF MOSES AND AARON: Moses and Aaron assembled the entire community before the rock and said to them impatiently: "Hear now, ye rebels; are we to bring you forth water out of this rock?" And Moses raised his rod and hit the rock with his staff twice. Immediately water flowed from the rock in great abundance, enough for the men and animals.

But Moses and Aaron had disobeyed G-d! Instead of *talking* to the stone, as they had been ordered to do, they had hit it with the staff. Thus, they had spoiled the opportunity to show the people that even a rock would obey G-d's command and give forth water, at the mere word of G-d. For Moses and Aaron, even this seemingly slight deviation from G-d's word was a grave and unpardonable sin. Their punishment was very grave, for G-d told them: "Because ye believed not in Me, to sanctify Me in the eyes of the children of Israel, ye shall not bring this assembly into the land which I have given them!"

Thereafter, the place where this had happened was called "May Meribah," the Waters of Strife, because there the children of Israel had quarreled with G-d for lack of water.

AARON'S DEATH: From Kadesh, the camp of the Jews travelled to Mount Hor. There G-d told Moses that Aaron was to die now. Moses took Aaron and his son Elazar, and together they ascended the mountain before the eyes of all Israel. In a cave near the peak of the mountain, Moses took the priestly robes off Aaron and put them on Elazar. Then Aaron lay down, and G-d took his holy soul back to heaven. Aaron was 123 years old when he died (on the first day of the month of Av, 2487). The death of Aaron was deeply mourned by all Israel.

THE BRAZEN SERPENT: After the children of Israel left Mount Hor, they had to journey all around the Land of Edom. Tired of travelling and marching, they again murmured bitterly against G-d and Moses. As a punishment G-d sent fiery serpents from whose sting many of the people died. Then they repented, and implored Moses to entreat G-d for pardon; he interceded, and his prayers were accepted by G-d. G-d commanded him to make a serpent of brass, and to place it upon a pole; and any man bitten by the fiery serpents who would look up to the brazen figure, as a symbol of his reliance on the Divine power and assistance, would be healed.

46. CONQUEST OF THE EAST OF THE JORDAN

THE CIRCUITOUS ROUTE: Finally, the children of Israel reached the frontiers of Edom, Ammon, and Moab, directly on their route to the Promised Land. But these nations refused to let the Jews pass through their countries. G-d forbade the children of Israel to make war upon these people. Therefore, the Jews had to march all around these countries, until they reached the River Arnon.

DEFEAT OF SIHON AND OG: From there Moses sent messengers to King Sihon of the Amorites, asking his permission for the children of Israel to pass through his land. Moses promised to use only the highway, and to make full reparations for any damage that might ensue. They would purchase their food and water from the natives.

Sihon refused this request and mobilized his entire army against the children of Israel. Sihon was defeated, and the children of Israel took possession of his entire country. The next king to challenge Israel was Og, the giant king of Bashan. He too was vanquished and slain by Moses, and his land passed into the hands of the children of Israel.

THE DIVISION OF TRANSJORDANIA: These two lands, the lands of the Amorites and of Bashan, were superbly suited for the raising of cattle and sheep. It so happened that the tribes of Reuben and Gad owned great numbers of flocks. Therefore, the leaders of these two tribes approached Moses and asked to be given the land of the Amorites and Bashan as their share of the conquest, instead of their due part in the land of Canaan, across the Jordan. Half the tribe of Manasseh joined the two tribes in their request. Reproachfully, Moses asked them whether they would have the nerve to sit by idly, watching their flocks, whilst their brethren would wage war against the natives of Canaan. But the men of Reuben, Gad and Manasseh assured Moses that not only would they fight shoulder to shoulder with the rest of Israel, but that they would also be in the forefront of the fight for the Holy Land. All they requested was that their families and flocks be permitted to remain on the east side of the Jordan till they returned after the complete conquest of Canaan. Moses agreed to this, and the women and children of these tribes of Israel were immediately settled in Transjordania. Their men, however, were among the vanguard of the Jewish troops. Only after the entire Holy Land had been conquered, did they return to their familes and flocks, to settle on their permanent heritage in Transjordania.

47. BALAAM AND BALAK

BALAK SENDS FOR BALAAM: Frightened by the fall of the lands of the Amorites and Bashan, the kings of Moab and Midian, implacable foes for many generations, united for the purpose of a common attack upon the children of Israel. Balak, the newly elected king of Moab, had been put in charge of the plans. Thinking of the surprising victories of the outnumbered troops of the Jewish people Balak came to the conclusion that these victories could only be attributed to some form of magic. He believed that the only way to destroy the victorious Jews was to outdo them in magic by a spell stronger than theirs.

Balak, therefore, sent messengers to Balaam, the greatest magician of those days, asking him to come to Moab to curse the people of Israel who were threatening to overrun their lands.

Balaam knew that he could not do anything against G-d's will, and he so informed Balak's envoys, even though his personal hatred of the Jews made him only too willing to follow the call.

However, Balak was persistent. He sent an even more imposing delegation of princes and nobles and promised Balaam more gold and silver. Balaam received the deputation with the respect due to their rank. Regretfully, he told them that even if Balak gave him a full house of gold and silver, he could not go against G-d's command. He asked them, however, to stay overnight, because only at night was he privileged to receive Divine inspiration. During that night, Balaam had a vision in which he was informed that he might go with Balak's men, but that he was not to say anything save the words that G-d would put into his mouth.

BALAAM'S ASS: Balaam rose early in the morning, saddled his ass, and went with the princes of Moab.

But G-d was angry at Balaam's eagerness to do harm to the Jewish people, and He sent an angel to hinder his way. The ass saw the angel of G-d with a drawn sword, and she tried to evade him by stepping off the path. Balaam, who did not perceive the angel, got angry and hit the ass in order to guide her back to the path. A little while later, the angel with the drawn sword blocked the way on a narrow vineyard path, fenced by walls on either side. Trying to avoid the angel, the ass pressed herself close to the wall, thereby hurting Balaam's foot. Again Balaam hit the ass. Now the angel placed himself squarely across the path where there was no chance of avoiding him, so this time the ass lay down, refusing to move forward. Now Balaam was in such a rage that he savagely hit the ass with his staff for the third time. At this moment, G-d gave the ass the faculty of speaking. The ass asked the astonished Balaam why he had beaten her these three times. Her master, stupefied, though still in a rage, replied that he would have killed her, had he only had a sword handy. Yet while Balaam spoke, G-d opened his eyes, and he saw the angel with the sword drawn in his hand. Balaam bowed in reverence. The Angel told Balaam that it was he who had blocked the way, and that Balaam had done an injustice to the ass. Balaam excused himself, saying that he had not known that G-d wanted to prevent his trip, and that he was ready to return. But the angel replied that he should continue his journey, remembering to say only that which G-d would tell him.

BALAAM'S BLESSINGS: When king Balak heard of Balaam's arrival, he went out to meet him and took the prophet up to the heights sacred to Baal. There they built seven altars, upon each of which they sacrificed an ox and a ram. Then Balaam went alone to a solitary place, hoping to receive the word of the Lord. When he returned to the king, he had beheld a vision, and he felt inspired. He stood near his burnt-offering before Balak and the princes of Moab, and urged by an irresistable impulse, he broke forth into blessings. "How shall I curse whom G-d hath not cursed?" Balaam exclaimed. He went on to praise the marvellous people which will never lose its identity among the nations of the world, and concluded with the words: "Let me die the death of the righteous, and let mine end be like his!"

Hearing Balaam's divinely inspired praise of Israel, Balak became angry at Balaam for blessing his enemies instead of cursing them. Balaam replied that he could say only what G-d put in his mouth.

Again Balak prepared sacrifices, and Balaam waited for an inspiration to curse the Jewish people. However, G-d put praise and blessings into his mouth. "G-d is not a man that He should lie. . . . When He hath said, will He not do it? Behold, I am bidden to bless; and when He hath blessed, I cannot call it back. None hath beheld iniquity in Jacob. Neither hath one seen perverseness in Israel; the Lord his G-d is with him. . . . "

The last time Balaam took a full view of Israel's camp, he exclaimed "How goodly are thy tents, O Jacob, thy dwellings, O Israel! As valleys stretch out, as gardens by the river-side; as aloes planted of the Lord, as cedars beside the waters. Water shall flow from his branches, and his seed shall be in many waters; and his king shall be higher than Agag, and his kingdom shall be exalted. G-d who brought him forth out of Egypt is for him like the lofty horns of the wild-ox; he shall eat up the nations that are his adversaries, and shall break their bones in pieces, and pierce them through with his arrows. He couched, he lay down as a lion, and as a lioness; who shall rouse him up? Blessed be every one that blesseth thee, and cursed be every one that curseth thee."

Now Balak was really angry, and he ordered Balaam to return home. Before he left, however, Balaam told Balak that the only way to harm the people of Israel was to seduce them into sin. For only then would G-d punish His people.

The kings of Moab and Midian acted upon this shrewd advice of Balaam. They arranged a big feast in honor of their idols and invited the children of Israel to participate in the ceremonies. Many of the Jewish people fell for this ruse and participated in these heathen celebrations. Amongst them was Zimri, a prince of the family of Simeon, who was not ashamed to let the entire Jewish community witness his evil conduct.

PINEHAS CHAMPIONS THE HONOR OF G-D: Pinehas, the son of Elazar the high priest, was among those who saw Zimri's shameless conduct. In his zeal to defend th honor of the Torah, he took a spear and entered Zimri's tent. Finding the ignoble prince in the company of the daughter of a Midianite prince, he killed them both with one thrust of his spear.

By this brave act, Pinehas stopped the plague which had begun among the children of Israel, and which had taken a toll of many thousands of dead among those who had allowed themselves to be seduced by the Midianites.

Pinehas' action was rewarded by a Divine covenant of peace and everlasting priesthood.

Following the outrageous attempt by the Midianites to seduce the children of Israel into sin, G-d ordered Moses to declare war against the Midianites and smite them. In the ensuing battle not only did the five princes of Midian fall with their vanquished troops, but also Balaam, the instigator of all this trouble, was slain.

48. MOSES' DEATH

END OF THE DESERT JOURNEY: When the children of Israel arrived at the Jordan, facing the city of Jericho, G-d ordered them to be counted. There were more than 600,000 men over twenty years, besides the members of the families of Levi. Among the adults there was not one, except Joshua and Caleb, who had been older than twenty years at the time of the exodus from Egypt. All the older generation had died in the desert, during the forty years' wandering, as G-d had decreed, in punishment for their rebellion.

INSTALLATION OF JOSHUA: At that time, G-d told Moses to go up to the mountain of Abarim and see the Promised Land, for like his brother Aaron, he was not to enter the Promised Land, because they had disobeyed G-d's order in the Desert of Zin.

Moses then asked for a successor to lead the children of Israel into the Promised Land, and G-d pointed to his disciple Joshua. G-d ordered Moses to put his hands on Joshua's head to invest him with full authority of leadership, and to present him to Elazar and the entire community. Moses could now die in peace, satisfied that his beloved flock would have a worthy shepherd.

MOSES' FAREWELL: On the first day of the eleventh month in the fortieth year after the exodus from Egypt, Moses began to review the entire Torah with the children of Israel. He reprimanded them for their sins against G-d, and exhorted them to observe His holy commands for all time to come. Calling upon heaven and earth to bear witness, Moses warned the people of Israel of the inevitable doom that would befall them in the event that they forsook the Torah and disregarded G-d's commands. They would then lose their land, their homes, their independence, and would be hunted and per-secuted by a cruel world. But never would G-d forsake them entirely. At the height of their sufferings, they would turn to G-d again, and He would save them from extinction and return them to a glory greater than before.

Moses wrote down the entire five books of the Penta-teuch, word for word, as dictated to him by G-d. This scroll of the Torah was put into the Holy Ark, next to the Tables of Testimony.

MOSES' DEATH: Moses blessed the people of Israel for the last time, and ascended the mountain of Nebo on the seventh day of Adar in the year 2488. He stood on top of Pisgah across Jericho and looked upon the Holy Land, for which he had longed all his life, but which by G-d's order, he was never to enter. Thus died Moses, G-d's faithful servant and Israel's loyal shepherd, in the land of Moab, in full view of the Holy land, towards which he had led the children of Israel during forty years of wandering through the desert. Moses was 120 years old when he died.

Moses was the greatest of men. His prophecy was of a higher order than that of all other prophets. He was closer to G-d than any human being ever was. G-d Himself took his holy soul to heaven and buried his body in a cave, hidden from all human eyes.

For thirty days, the children of Israel mourned the death of their greatest leader. But they did not fall into de-spair, for left to lead them was a worthy successor to Moses, his devout disciple—Joshua.

END OF BOOK TWO

TEST YOUR KNOWLEDGE

1. How long did the children of Israel remain encamped at Mt. Sinai? (p. 135)

2. Who were Eldad and Medad? (p. 136)

3. Why was Miriam smitten with leprosy? (p. 137)

4. How long were the "Scouts" on their way? (p. 138)

5. What happened in the desert on the night of Tisha B'Av? (p. 139)

6. Name the two scouts who did not share in the evil report? (p. 139)

7. Who was Tzelophehad? (p. 141)

8. What relative of Moses fomented a serious rebellion against him? (p. 142)

9. Who were Dathan and Abiram? (p. 143)

10. How was Aaron's authority finally proved? (p. 144)

11. What misfortune followed Miriam's death? (p. 145)

12. What occurred in Kadesh? (p. 146)

13. What occurred on Mount Hor? (p. 146)

14. How was Transjordania divided? (p. 148)

15. Who said "How goodly are thy tents, O Jacob!"? (p. 151)

16. What made Pinehas famous? (p. 152)

17. Who was chosen to succeed Moses? (p. 153)

18. What final acts did Moses do before his death? (pp. 153, 154)

SUPPLEMENT

EVENTS & DATES

Event: *Year After Creation*:

FROM THE CREATION TO ABRAHAM *
(Chapters 1-8)

Adam	1 - 930
Noah	1056 - 2006
The Flood	1656
The Tower of Babel	1996

ABRAHAM AND SARAH (Chapters 9-11)

Abram born	1948
Sarai born	1958
The Covenant	2018
Abram and all his family go to Canaan	2023
Ishmael born	2034
Change of names to Abraham and Sarah; *Brith-milah* of Abraham and his household	2047
Destruction of Sodom	2047
Isaac born	2048
Sarah dies	2085
Abraham dies	2123

ISAAC AND REBEKAH (Chapters 12-15)

Isaac born	2048
The Binding of Isaac (Akedah)	2085
Marriage of Isaac and Rebekah	2088
Jacob and Esau born	2108
Rebekah dies	2207
Isaac dies	2228

JACOB AND THE TRIBES (Chapters 16-26)

Jacob born	2108
Isaac blesses Jacob	2171
Jacob resumes studies at Academy of Eber	2171 - 2185
Jacob goes to Haran	2185
Jacob married	2192
Tribes (except Joseph and Benjamin) born	2193 - 2198
Joseph born	2199
Jacob returns to Canaan; Benjamin born	2207 - 2208
Joseph sold	2216
Joseph becomes Grand Vizier of Egypt	2229
Jacob and his family come to Egypt	2238
Jacob dies	2255
Joseph dies	2309
Levi dies, last of the Tribes	2331 or 2332

---

* See Chart (p. 160) for detailed dates for this period.

Event:		Year After Creation:

THE CHILDREN OF ISRAEL IN EGYPT
(*Chapters* 27-32)

Jacob and his family come to Egypt		2238
Levi dies, last of the tribes: Beginning of the oppression in Egypt		2331 or 2332
Beginning of enslavement of the children of Israel in Egypt		2362 or 2363
Moses born		2368
Moses appears before Pharaoh demanding the release of Israel from Egypt		2447
The Exodus of Israel from Egypt	Nissan 15	2448

THE EXODUS AND REVELATION ON MT. SINAI   (*Chapters* 33-39)

The departure from Egypt	Nissan 15	2448
Passage through the Red Sea	Nissan 21	2448
The Manna begins	Iyar 16	2448
The Giving of the Torah on Mt. Sinai	Sivan 6	2448
The 'Golden Calf' made	Tammuz 16	2448
Moses descends from Mt. Sinai breaks the First Tablets	Tammuz 17	2448
Moses descends from Mt. Sinai for the third time (Yom Kippur)	Tishri 10	2448
Beginning of the contributions towards the building of the Mishkan (a day after Yom Kippur)	Tishri 11	2449

THE CHILDREN OF ISRAEL IN THE DESERT
(*Chapters* 40-48)

Erection of the Mishkan	Nissan 1	2449
Offerings of the princes upon the dedication of the Mishkan	Nissan 1 to 12	2449
First Red Heifer	Nissan 2	2449
First *Pesach* in the desert	Nissan 14	2449
Enumeration of the children of Israel in the desert	Iyar 1	2449
First *Pesach-sheni*	Iyar 14	2449
Children of Israel journey forth from the desert of Sinai	Iyar 20	2449
The scouts sent to the land of Canaan	Sivan 29	2449
The scouts return; rebellion	Ab 9	2449
Miriam the prophetess dies	Nissan 10	2487
Aaron the High Priest dies	Ab 1	2487
Moses dies	Adar 7	2488

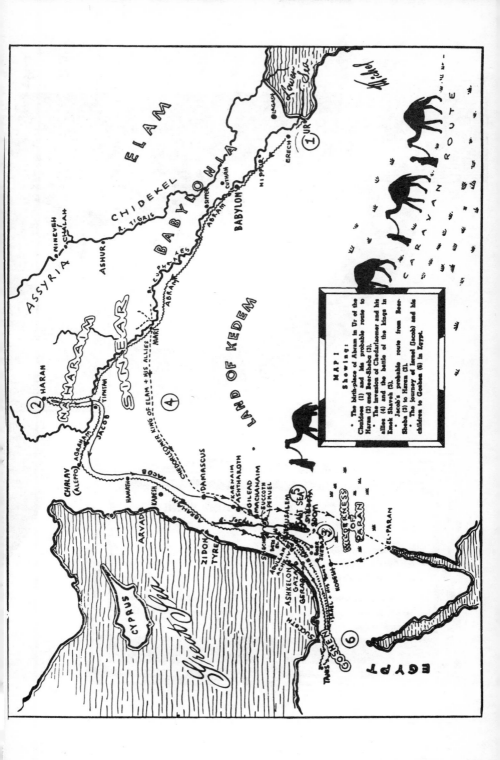

MAP I
Showing:
• The birth-place of Abram in Ur of the Chaldees (1) and his probable route to Haran (2) and Beer-Sheba (3).
• The invasion of Chedarlaomer and his allies (4) and the battle of the kings in Emek Shaveh (5).
• Jacob's probable route from Beer-Sheba (3) to Haran (2).
• The journey of Israel (Jacob) and his children to Goshen (6) in Egypt.

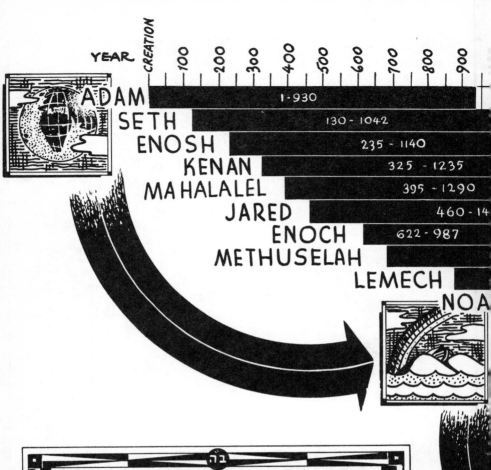

YEAR · CREATION · 100 · 200 · 300 · 400 · 500 · 600 · 700 · 800 · 900

ADAM 1-930
SETH 130 - 1042
ENOSH 235 - 1140
KENAN 325 - 1235
MAHALALEL 395 - 1290
JARED 460 - 14
ENOCH 622 - 987
METHUSELAH
LEMECH
NOA

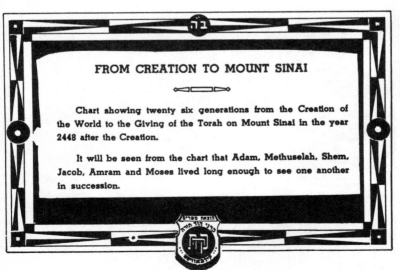

FROM CREATION TO MOUNT SINAI

◁━━▷

   Chart showing twenty six generations from the Creation of the World to the Giving of the Torah on Mount Sinai in the year 2448 after the Creation.

   It will be seen from the chart that Adam, Methuselah, Shem, Jacob, Amram and Moses lived long enough to see one another in succession.

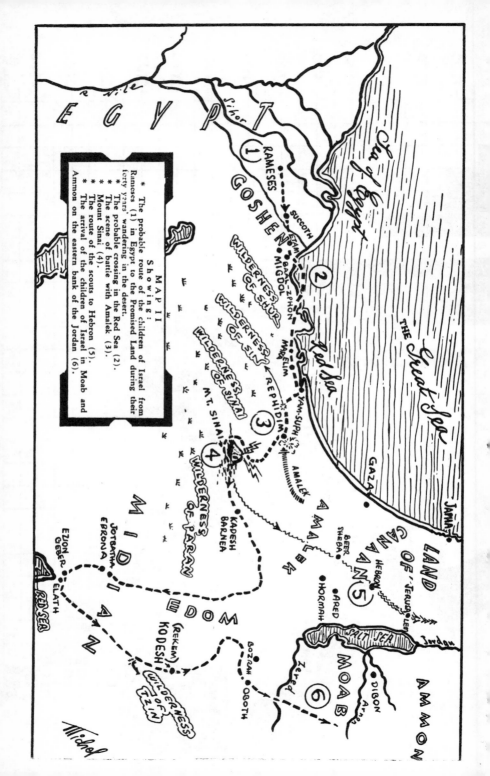

MAP II
Showing:

* The probable route of the children of Israel from Rameses (1) in Egypt to the Promised Land during their forty years' wandering in the desert.
* The probable crossing in the Red Sea (2).
* The scene of battle with Amalek (3).
* Mount Sinai (4).
* The route of the scouts to Hebron (5).
* The arrival of the children of Israel in Moab and Ammon on the eastern bank of the Jordan (6).

INDEX OF NAMES AND PLACES

INDEX OF NAMES AND PLACES